SEEDS

SEEDS

Stan Drew, Jr.

XULON PRESS ELITE

Xulon Press Elite
2301 Lucien Way #415
Maitland, FL 32751
407.339.4217
www.xulonpress.com

© 2020 by Stan Drew, Jr.

All rights reserved solely by the author. The author guarantees all contents are original and do not infringe upon the legal rights of any other person or work. No part of this book may be reproduced in any form without the permission of the author. The views expressed in this book are not necessarily those of the publisher.

Unless otherwise indicated, Scripture quotations taken from the Holy Bible, New International Version (NIV). Copyright © 1973, 1978, 1984, 2011 by Biblica, Inc.™. Used by permission. All rights reserved.

Scripture quotations taken from the King James Version (KJV)–*public domain*.

Scripture quotations taken from the New King James Version (NKJV). Copyright © 1982 by Thomas Nelson, Inc. Used by permission. All rights reserved.

Printed in the United States of America.

Paperback ISBN-13: 978-1-6322-1078-4
Hardcover ISBN-13: 978-1-6322-1079-1
eBook ISBN-13: 978-1-6322-1080-7

Foreword

I MET STAN DREW some 15 years ago in a barbecue restaurant in South Florida. After overhearing his conversations with customers and staff, it turns out we were both making efforts to witness to the people there.

I knew right away, this man had a true heart for Jesus Christ, and that he didn't just speak "Christianese." He was argumentative when he had to be, particularly in his defense of biblical principles. He was bold to say the least, and he always enjoyed discussions beyond the normal realm of the "religious." Yet he spoke in terms others could understand.

For at least ten years following that meeting, we had lunch together nearly every day and became fast friends. We talked about life, fishing, our work, but mostly we talked about the things of God. We both enjoyed sharing what we knew and learning from the process. It was the place of iron sharpening iron. As a result of our conversations, we grew as Christians.

Stan doesn't talk about religion. He talks about God. No one person has affected me more in my life. I am proud to call him friend. I know that feeling is mutual.

I could tell you a lot of stories but the truth is, there's a lot of them in the book. So read his book. It'll be a lot of fun! He means what he says and he loves the Lord.

*Send the twenty bucks for writing this in cash, Stan…

-Mark Hightower Friend,
 Design Engineer, Pickle baller,
 Christian, and Fisherman, Extraordinaire

Introduction

I BELIEVE THIS IS the part where I bow deeply at the waist and introduce myself. My name is of course, written on the cover of this work, so no sense repeating that. My photo is on the back. It has to be so those who know me will be certain that indeed, I am the author. That arrangement is as it should be. I am certain that some from my past will make the "Nah, couldn't be..." comment but that's the beauty of living longer than anyone expected.

Having no particular claim to fame, I have already engaged you personally, which is the stuff of marketing geniuses and the hand of a particularly generous and loving God.

It almost feels like an imposition to enter your world and mingle with the other folks in your mind. I trust this encounter will be a welcome one. That is my intention, though sometimes due to aging, arthritic bones, inclement weather and the ability of others to be rude, I tend to be a bit shall we say, cantankerous.

This entire adventure began as simple messages to friends and family on social media. I had no idea that a book would follow... nor did I realize that God himself was calling me into service.

This is a book that took in the neighborhood of ten years to write. It is a collection of musings, remembrances, silly moments, rants and very, very serious encounters with the God of the bible.

I trust my own human nature will not detract from the reality of anyone considering a relationship with the living God. To suppress my own senses of humor, outrage and sometimes callousness, would be deceitful if indeed, I allege to be writing from all four chambers of the heart.

Call this a history of my personal Damascus Road encounter. Meeting this Jesus in the middle of an ongoing train wreck was not something I expected, certainly not something I went about the business of pursuing.

I'm not a religious man as the world views religious men. I am a layman, a student of God and an aging rounder, capable still of causing a ruckus if indeed dust needs to be stirred. I am generally a man of peace, comfortable in my own blotchy skin and willing to discuss the things of heaven with anyone, for the most part.

I am not as recovered from the world as I am aware of the evil that exists in it. That may be the very reason my road was a bit rocky. My response to the world at large was to befriend the whole of it and indulge in all it had to offer. I am, in the truest sense of the word, blessed to be here.

I haven't an ounce of excuse for remaining on the planet this long. It certainly was not my intent. I expected a shorter existence but it appears God had different plans. Indeed, it is His plan that sets the boundaries, like it or not.

Suffice to say, listening is not my strong suit. I'm sure my wife would agree. I'm sure my parents would have agreed. I'd venture to say that teachers, preachers, drill instructors, bosses and a host of government clerks would all agree...I would imagine then, that the overall consensus is that I don't listen well.

So, how could I possibly have heard the still, small voice of God? Better yet, how could I have become the slightest bit trusting of that voice and, more than any other question, where did this sudden burst of humility begin? The answer to that lies in my own weakness, and the power of God to not only transform a heart but to make a completely new creature from a self-involved, hostile rebel of the Dixie sort...Potter meet clay and vice versa.

It is important to note at this point, that the condition of the world matters to me. It matters enough to write about it...not just about my life experience while engaged with it but to also expose my thoughts and make an effort to tell others what they need to hear from one who embraced the wrong cause. I trust God will use this book to whisper in someone's ear, "Come unto me."

It is not necessarily a Christian book, though it falls into that genre. If that definition assumes that the writer is Christian, that is true. However, it isn't written to just other Christians. It is an honest effort to engage others outside the Christian hive with the truths I have learned as one who operated outside the realm of Christian thinking. If sweat equity is a real thing, I have invested much in this, my first book.

After much back and forth, damning insecurities about exposing myself and a host of other reasons to not write the book, I prayed specifically about it for far too long a period of time. It became clear that there was indeed a reason for the book and an audience beyond what I could expect. I finally gained the proper perspective that if even one person was touched by my effort, then it was indeed treasure in heaven. That said, I took the "Thy will be done." option, which is never really an option, but I digress.

I began sorting through my collection of vignettes and landed in a place I believe others will find encouraging and hopefully interesting enough to cause them to read this work in its entirety. The effort was to be able to open the book and receive a short burst of encouragement or inspiration or even humor. I can only hope this was accomplished.

The Map...

THE SUREST WAY to navigate a collection of this sort is to identify, then classify each entry. In that effort, the following categories were used to identify each offering. There is no particular order of precedent to the entries scattered throughout the book. They are each a moment, a thought...seeds, if you will...personal testimonies and observances of the God of creation, along with excerpts from my own experiences.

I trust some of these seeds will land on fertile soil and cause at least a glance in the direction of heaven. I can only hope to offer some level of enjoyment to those who choose to read it. I have used the following icons to distinguish the attitude of these various entries. The symbol indicates the premise of each entry...

Thoughtful

Perspectives

Personal

Blessings

Poetry

Tales

Light hearted

Patriotic

Let's get it over with…Here's the actual story…

Back in 2016, when this whole kneeling thing kicked up, I was a bit perturbed at these folks who, by virtue of their celebrity sports figure status, decided it was a smart thing to do to kneel while the United States flag was being displayed and the anthem being played.

There are a few things that just aren't acceptable to me and apparently, a lot of others… There is literally no reason to disrespect the symbol of American pride revered by so many. There is a higher honor reserved for those who've shed blood for this country. I don't really care how anyone else views that. Offending veterans and the families of heroes just isn't an acceptable method for protest. Its just an insult. I have a folded flag in my living room. It was on my dad's casket. It's a memory of his service. I too served. I'm not amenable to anyone's idea of what it represents. I know what it represents. If you don't, that's on you.

Needless to say, I mulled it over for a while and it started to get to me, so I wrote a piece as a response to this act that I believe still to be shameful…Call me crazy.

Without belaboring the point, it seems that a celebrity guitarist received the piece and copied and pasted it to his own site. He, being a spokesman for conservative thought, then proceeded to go on tour to Japan. He cut and pasted the piece rather than sharing it. That is a pretty common mistake but what that actually does is exactly what it did. It makes the post look as if the person reposting it wrote the piece. I have to admit, that was a pretty deep wound but there are two ways to look at that. I could look at it as an attempt to plagiarize my work…or I could accept that the piece would never have gained the traction it did unless someone with a couple of million friends posted it without knowing the author.

The piece went viral…Super viral…Apparently it hit an American nerve. Everyone thought he wrote it but due to some absolutely tenacious friends and family, we started to correct the piece just about everywhere it travelled. The media even picked it up and wrote articles about the assumed author.

To my knowledge (We've never spoken) He was completely unaware that the writing had received over 100,000 hits and a lot of commentary. I'm sure he wasn't interested in checking his social media pages while on tour in Japan, so the article and the credit for it continued to gather steam until such time as he returned home. The press began their usual one-sided assault and wrote various articles about the now incendiary work.

We continued to respond to the error on social media accounts to no avail. In doing so, a former singer of some renown (who will also remain nameless due to his recent demise) contacted me and told me that he had the artist's personal number and would speak to him about the inadvertent attribution. He did just that and it wasn't long before my name miraculously appeared at the bottom of my now famous editorial.

Of course, the majority of the credit was still going to the famed musician and the circulation of the piece shared from his account was multiplied into the millions. It still comes around every Memorial Day, Veterans Day and anytime one of these millionaire superstars decides it's still a good idea to dishonor the American flag. I still have people faithful to the cause of correcting the accidental author misattribution. At this point, it's just good to know that so many have read something I wrote even if it has been attributed to another author.

As of this writing. The artists people have denied that he ever wrote the article, so I guess there is solace in that. In fact, whenever the article is presented, if it is indeed the one that carries his name as the author, it is covered by a fact check box stating that it has been debunked. Only the misattribution was debunked. The piece itself is as true as the day I wrote it. Clearly though, the politics have changed and I'm sure kneeling will once again be all the rage. I for one, will not deny the essence nor the reason for the writing. I'm still as proud of it as the day I wrote it, as I am of this America.

I thought it best to present it as the first piece in my book. That way, we can preclude any challenges to the rest of my writing. It is now officially, a genuine excerpt from my book.

So, without further ado…

So, You Want to Take a Knee?

TAKE A LITTLE trip to Valley Forge in January. If you don't know where that is, just Google it from the sidelines. Hold a musket ball in your fingers and imagine it piercing your flesh and breaking a bone or two. There won't be a doctor or trainer to assist you until after the battle, so just wait your turn. Take your cleats and socks off to get a real experience. Then take a knee.

Then, take one at the beach in Normandy where man after American man stormed the beach, even as the one in front of him was shot to pieces...the very sea stained with American blood. The only blockers most had were the dead bodies in front of them, riddled with bullets from enemy fire.

Take a knee in the sweat soaked jungles of Vietnam. from Khe Sanh to Saigon...Anywhere will do. Americans died in all those jungles. There was no playbook that told them what was next, but they knew what flag they represented When they came home, they were protested as well, and spit on for reasons only cowards know.

Take another knee in the blood drenched sands of Fallujah in 110-degree heat. Wear your Kevlar helmet and battle dress...Your number won't be printed on it unless your number is up! You'll need to stay hydrated but there won't be anyone to squirt Gatorade into your mouth. You're on your own.

There's a lot of places to take a knee. Americans have given their lives all over the world. When you use the banner under which they fought as a source for your displeasure, you dishonor the memories of those who bled for the very freedoms you have.

That's what the red stripes mean. They represent the blood of those who spilled a sea of it defending your liberty.

While you're on your knee, thank Almighty God for those that came before you, not on a manicured lawn striped and printed with numbers to announce every inch of ground taken...but on nameless hills and bloodied beaches and sweltering forests and bitter cold mountains...every inch marked by an American life lost serving that flag you protest.

No cheerleaders, no announcers, no coaches, no fans...just American men and women...delivering the real fight against those who chose to harm us...blazing a path so you would have the right to "take a knee."

You haven't an inkling what it took to get you where you are...but your "protest" is duly noted. Not only is it disgraceful to a nation of real heroes, it serves the purpose of pointing to your ingratitude for those who chose to defend you under that banner that will still wave long after your jersey is retired...

If you really feel the need to take a knee, come with me to church on Sunday and we'll both kneel before Almighty God. We'll thank him for preserving this country for as long as He has. We'll beg forgiveness for our ingratitude for all He has provided us. We'll appeal to Him for understanding and wisdom. We'll pray for liberty and justice for all...because He is the one who provides those things.

But there will be no protest. There will only be gratitude for His provision and a plea for His continued grace and mercy on the land of the free and the home of the brave. It goes like this...

GOD BLESS AMERICA!

Unashamed

I DON'T CONSIDER MYSELF particularly insightful just because I can string together a few sentences and make a legitimate argument about the things of God. The most frustrating part of that is not being able to lead all the horses to drink.

I'm not a theologian but I study the bible. I listen to sermons and try to relate to the world around me without pointing fingers. That's my job. It's what I do.

It's becoming more and more difficult to communicate with the otherwise "educated." I see overall education as a lost cause though the arts still show promise as well as the sciences and specifically defined areas. I do believe though, that indoctrination is becoming a viable replacement for efforts in the areas of humanities...philosophy, law, politics, etc. It seems that everyone leaves those environments with the same set of principles and an aversion to the things of God.

I have some very bright friends. They all say the same thing... We're losing. Christianity itself is losing the argument. There are a lot of reasons for that, some I can even agree with but taking it all to its ultimate end, I can't seem to walk the spiritually unequipped to a place of understanding what this "God thing" is all about.

I don't want to believe that they are blinded, or that their heart is spiritually hardened...or that they have been "given over to reprobate minds"...but I simply cannot construct an argument that causes them to accept the reality, or even the possibility that God exists and that He is worth knowing. There is a virtual wall that prevents some of these conversations from developing. I'm sure I know who the builder of that wall is...personally! We've met!

It's all very subtle. I'm not invited to a lot of places because it's pretty well known that I don't necessarily engage socially in the way others expect. I am unabashedly Christian...unashamed of the gospel. At least I am in my own mind...and I depend on "the hope that lies within me" to move past those walls. Sometimes that takes more time than I have. The arguments are ancient, as is the message of the gospel of Jesus Christ.

Every normal conversation becomes difficult because I can almost feel the weight of the elephant in the room. "Is he going to talk about Jesus...Again? Oh please no... He really believes that stuff and I know he's sincere, but no... Please no!"

The weight of that conversation is more on others than it is on me...I don't generally bring it up but sometimes, all roads lead to that "uncomfortable" place. I don't want to put anyone on the spot or engage them before they're ready...so I don't. I believe that those discussions will come naturally. I believe that God will guide all of them.

As with everything, I trust that God will cause those conversations. It's not for me to demand to be heard. I'm not that impolite or socially ignorant. Planting seeds is a quiet job. I realize that tilling the soil is disruptive.

Still, in any social environment, particularly those where people know me, there seems to be a fear that I might suddenly rise from my chair, tink on a glass with my spoon and announce the coming apocalypse...locusts and pestilence and a pox on your houses..."Y'all goin ta' hell for watchin' them dancin' girls at the Superbowl," ain't exactly my style.

That's not generally how an eternal conversation happens and of course, we as believers dread those types of conversations more than the average non believer. Suffice to say I'd really like to answer your questions about my relationship with the Lord. I can't do that while I'm preaching and foaming at the mouth, which isn't really my style either, particularly if you have preconceived notions about my intent...so you should know that I'm approachable. Intimidation is not my method. Hopefully, reason comes into play...because God wants us to be reasonable...even with Him.

Mostly though, I'd like to live a life that you find interesting...not overly pious or hard-nosed with regard to my "religious views."... not ignoring the message but certainly not "cramming anything down your throat."

I hope that same message comes across in my writing...that I care enough about you to talk to you about Jesus in a loving, personal way ...without having to slam the car door on your coat to get you to stay...

If all you have for me is insult, that's on you...I'll politely, if at all possible, excuse myself from all the foolishness that follows... but if you want to have a conversation about what I believe and why I believe it, I trust I will be more than accommodating. I do not fear that conversation. I do not fear the place where I stand because there is no firmer foundation!

>Romans 1:16
>"For I am not ashamed of the gospel, because it is the power of God that brings."

Testing in Progress

Not that I'm the I'm arbiter of goodness or the sole judge of what is and isn't deceitful...not even close...but I have learned to ask myself, why I think what I think. It gets easier as I practice.

First, I ask myself "Why am I even thinking about this?"...Has a news item or a commercial or some other stimulus caused me to think about a certain thing? We are under a barrage of media almost constantly...so it's important to know what it is that kick starts our thinking processes.

The next thing I ask is "Was it intentional?"... Where did the thought originate? Was the thought planted and was it constructed in such a way as to cause me to lean one way or the other...In other words, is there subliminal motivation? There's a lot of effort that goes into messaging these days so I try to distance myself from the marketing geniuses and make up my mind about " things" without too much interference.

Many times, when watching the broadcast news on tv. or searching internet stories, I see and hear folks presenting their case without an ounce of evidence...or even a structured statement or a supported fact...just a random " because I said it here, it must be true." We all see that when we turn to the channel or go to the site that glaringly offers an opinion that opposes our own...We just know it's wrong...but how do we know?

Anytime I hear catch phrases like "anonymous sources" or a "spokesman for the (whatever)...or that "(whomever) was unavailable for comment"...or if a story immediately blames an opposing force (i.e. Republican...liberal...yada yada) I have to question the integrity of that commentary...and the spirit in which it is offered...particularly since everything seems to be politicized these days.

Questioning or "discerning" spirits relates to the underlying motivation...Does it come from an evil place...or does it have good intent? Is it honest? Is it something I should get on board with...or should I investigate further? A good question to ask is always " Is it productive or destructive?"... Another is "Does it have eternal value?" Questioning intent is a true "testing"...and necessary to keep us from becoming one of the programmed...

Proper discernment assists us in maintaining our spiritual balance...

As Christians, we are required to "Seek first the kingdom of God." So, there's the starting point...Seek God's motivation first...Pray and read the bible...before the bombardment begins.

> *1 John 4:1*
> *Beloved, do not believe every spirit, but test the spirits whether they are from God, for many false prophets have gone out into the world.*

As a Matter of Fact

ONE OF THE reasons I write is to relieve tension...Like anyone, I see and hear far too much media...I keep my distance but I try to keep "plugged in" enough to stay current...

The problem with that is, staying current means that I have to be aware of all the various attempts by media to promote ideas that are antithetical to what I believe. I dodge most of it more often than not, but still it slithers in, ever creeping, nudging forward, producing plagues of the mind that literally have no element of truth..."facts" so altered that to argue against them is an exercise in remedial thinking. I find myself asking for the most part, "Where do they get this stuff...and how is it they have come to believe it?"

Without any spiritual discernment, I could easily be convinced that some of the present-day ideas are more valuable than they really are...I could accept politically generated redefinitions as wholly responsible, well thought out, educated certainties...but I don't...because they aren't. They're missing the most important element of truth.

I could, without prayerful consideration, be convinced that certain moral attitudes are acceptable to God, because of how they are presented, mostly using "fairness" or "equality" as the standard for measurement. However, subtle coercion is still coercion... Being convinced through a barrage of media is no way to discern the truth from a lie. It doesn't require a "panel of experts" to decide truth.

So, what makes me the arbiter of truth? How do I go about the business of understanding what is and isn't true? How do I effectively "snope" the truth? (not that I accept Snopes as the measurement of truth...but it has become the preeminent "go to" for "factual" accounting...Hence, the metaphor.)

Indeed, it is necessary for me to "plug into" antiquity in order to maintain balance...Rather than a moral compass, I need a moral gyroscope to stay the course...I cannot, with any degree of certainty, intellectually distinguish truth from a lie without some inward GPS...some way of locating the truth in the midst of so many avenues of approach...What is the delivery system by which I can be assured that I am gaining knowledge of the truth?

Foundational truth lies in the Word of God. The truth is revealed as we seek God through the Scriptures...So how is that word interpreted? As we read and study, we are enlightened by God himself...The Holy Spirit, who indwells us the moment we accept Jesus Christ as our savior...guards our hearts and guides us in the way that we should go...Thus, the "Snopes" that lies within me...

We can, with His assistance, determine truth. Otherwise, we have only our human intellect and the constant bombardment of outside stimuli to distinguish what is and isn't truth...Those human attributes alone will invariably fail.

> *1 John 5:6*
> *"And it is the Spirit who bears witness, because the Spirit is the truth."*

Geniusis

WHAT IS THAT force that causes a heart to beat, not just once but synchronized in time with all of creation, for as long as it takes to serve the purpose for which it was designed?

What causes a flower to bloom, a leaf to change color, a mountain to explode, a star to die, a universe to expand, opens a baby's clenched fist and closes it around its mother's finger?

By what measure do we explain a first breath, winged flight, gravitational pull, cellular activity?

What is that unseen energy that causes a wave to crest again and again, a shadow to form, a bird to sing? What causes a moment to pass?

What discipline demands an orbit, or twists a strand of DNA... or colors the sunrise? What floats a cloud, calls down the wind, moves the sand from one place to the next?

How balanced is the sun with the stars and to what do we owe the pleasure of its warmth or the wealth of its light?

What metronomic agency times the seasons, refreshes the streams, balances the seas and calms the storms? And who are you to tell us? By who's authority do you answer? Would you indeed usurp the power of the living God to display your great knowledge?

How then, do you know what is evil and what is good, but mostly how do you expect to teach me? How is it that you convince me that you are the arbiter of such things? Are you not made of the same flesh and bones?

How great we have become...How noble our cause...How deep our understanding...

Still, our bodies return to dust and our souls to eternity, demanding the one who made us to show Himself, ignoring the evidences of His purposed and immense design.

Indeed, how great we aren't...

> *Roman's 1:20*
> *For ever since the world was created, people have seen the earth and sky. Through everything God made, they can clearly see his invisible qualities—his eternal power and divine nature. So, they have no excuse for not knowing God.*

Think-tanked

So, I was thinking...a somewhat dangerous effort these days as I hadn't even turned on the TV to find out what exactly I was supposed to be thinking...

My wife was still asleep so I went about the business of finding my way to the family room without disturbing the quiet...the rubber tip on my cane sounding more like a video game than an assisting device...You'd think I'd know the way by now but the early morning journey is nearly always interrupted by a bump or a creak or a light left off by mistake.

In an uncharacteristic gesture, I reached for my Bible before I realized that I had left my phone charging in the bedroom and had inadvertently failed to push the power button on my computer...I was literally alone with my thoughts...a blank canvas...mentally detached from all the stimuli that ignites my thought processes...

So, there I was...alone in the dark with the book...clearing the fog, as it were...not really concentrating, still in need of caffeine, reeling from the complications of a restless night's sleep...not really nightmarish...just complicated scenes.

Staring at the pages as I thumbed to the marker from yesterday, I came across this highlighted passage...one I had read hundreds of times...

"Finally, brothers and sisters, whatever is true, whatever is noble, whatever is right, whatever is pure, whatever is lovely, whatever is

admirable—if anything is excellent or praiseworthy—think about such things." -Philippians 4:8

I imagined what it would be like to spend my day actually doing that...I delighted in the virtue of it...but ignored the possibility because there's just not that much good in the world; not a lot noble or right, or pure...except maybe pure evil, but lovely? admirable? excellent? praiseworthy?... Really?

Then I flicked on the TV, cranked up the computer and started making coffee...laughing at myself for even considering such a thing...

That's when I heard about the murder and rape... and the war...the death and destruction...the children...the threats...the hostility...the political chest pounding...

Suddenly, I was comfortable in my own skin...the anxiousness and panic starting to seep into the inner recesses, clearing the cobwebs...my brain responding to the chatter...my eyes focused on scenes of war-torn deserts and riotous mobs...panels of experts demanding my full attention...politicians belittling other politicians...and so on...and so on...ad nauseam

Snapping the top off the plastic bottle, I down the blood pressure medication and go about the business of studying the lesson I had intended to study...ignoring the one God himself had placed directly in front of me...That is the nature of the beast...Responding to the noise rather than listening to the Shepherd...Thank you Lord, for pointing that out. You alone are worthy, holy, righteous, lovely, admirable, praiseworthy, noble, excellent, indeed!

Divin' Intervention

THIS IS A very long but true story...If you've got time to read it, then be my guest...If not, okay then...It's not a requirement for graduation...

In the summer of 1982, I was a soldier in the 1st year of my second enlistment. 2/24th mechanized Infantry. Ft. Stewart, Ga.

Just back from a long stint in Germany, I was back stateside just in time for field duty in the "Garden of the South"...My luck... Nothing like scraping caked on mud off your boots before your first inspection.

I remember it like it was yesterday...though the exact date escapes me...It was a slow-motion event that changed my life...There were stories and photographs about it in the local Savannah papers and an article in the Army Times. I'm telling it because it has flooded my mind for several days...and I can't shake it...I hope I never do... It doesn't haunt me...just the opposite...It soothes me...

I was driving an armored personnel carrier over the Canoochee River during Operation Mud flap (or something...We named all of them) I moved from the staggered position to fall in behind the vehicle in front of me, which actually is the tactical method for crossing a bridge.

As I pulled the lateral (steering mechanism) to make the slow turn to the left...it stuck a bit...I believe the lanyard (cord) attached to my .45 pistol had become entangled...I jerked back on the lateral in an effort to free it...This caused me to take an abrupt left... Not good...

From there a series of events occurred...I accelerated for no explicable reason...except that I most likely stood trying to yank the lanyard from the steering lateral which probably caused me to stand and press the accelerator...rather than release the laterals which would have brought me to a stop...so yep...I drove a 13 ton (mortar carrier) off a 20 foot high bridge...into a 30 foot deep, fast flowing river...

I remember the free fall and was able to determine rather quickly that this event probably wouldn't end well...Again...slow motion... The sudden silence from the tracks leaving the ground and being airborne was strange to say the least...like wheels up in a plane... from heavy clattering to swooshing air...

I remember entering the river head first, still gripping the laterals and the sudden rush of water all around...like riding a roller coaster, really...The sound was somewhere between a loud splash and a bubbling geyser...a "kerthunk splash" as it were (Sorry... best description I can muster.) The concussion was immense...as if riding the proverbial ton of bricks as they dropped into the river from a great height

I remember taking a deep breath as I entered the water...more of a gasp than an intentional breath...The back hatch was open as were both the drivers hatch and Tank Commander hatch. (I found out later, the TC had escaped while we were still on the bridge.)

I was upside down in the water, sinking quickly to the bottom...but inside, everything was normal. I remember seeing the radio lights behind me and the operating lights in front through the murky water…red and orange glowing lights…

I also remember distinctly saying…or maybe thinking… to God himself, "So this is it…Okay then!" I reflected on my parents and how sad they would be…and my then girlfriend, "Whatsername." I asked God (with whom I wasn't very close at the time) to watch over them.

I briefly, but frantically struggled to remove the entangled lanyard… Really though, all I had to do was unholster my weapon…Best decision I'd made all day…Then there was the Communications helmet…No problem there either.

The next moment was surreal…but it is as fixed in my mind as any other major decision… I decided to take a deep breath to expedite the process of drowning, rather than put off the obvious consequences of driving a large hunk of metal off a bridge…This wouldn't be very difficult as I was nearly out of air.

So, I went about the business of drowning…I wondered if taking the breath intentionally constituted a form of suicide. I held up a millisecond or so…or whatever time measurement is best suited to slow motion…but the decision was made.

I was calm…I could not understand why I wasn't completely freaked out. I figured I deserved this ending and accepted it like I would a gift. In a way, I was anxious to see what happened next… That thought sticks with me…The Bible says there is a "peace beyond understanding." That best describes my level of calm… almost serene…acceptance.

I loved life!...Ask anyone who knew me then! I simply regarded this ending as appropriate...and knew I'd had a good run...I was completely acceptant that this accident was not survivable...Better this than dying of hunger or burning to death...or having to explain this particular event to my 1st Sergeant...Suffice to say I accepted it at face value...Still, I was incredibly calm...Mostly, I was aware that I was calm and that life as I knew it, would soon be over

I tried not to reflect on my life though I can attest to the "flashing by" of it...because I knew how badly I had lived it...I knew how disappointed Jesus must be in me...I was still going to enjoy meeting him...This thought absolutely pervaded any other thought.

I had a bit of a flashback, I guess...I remembered walking down the church aisle when I was twelve and "giving my life to the Lord"... never actually sure of what that meant...but aware at this moment that I was his...to do with as he wanted...Somehow, I knew that hell would have none of me...It was reassuring in an inexplicable way...Death, as it was called, was a breath away...

Then Bubbles...Lots of bubbles...Big ones that I could follow all the way to the surface...That's when I realized I could see the surface...All the murky rushing water had settled but it was a good twenty feet above... I didn't really know how I had gotten right side up...One moment I was still gripping the laterals upside down...the next, I could see the surface. Just as time had slowed, so had distance expanded...I couldn't possibly have enough breath to reach the surface...It seemed impossible to span that distance with so little breath...Not gonna' happen...I conceded...

Then, without any notice, I was floating... Apparently, I had floated out of the open hatch...which had somehow allowed me to float free...I had done nothing on my own to free myself outside of losing the pistol and helmet...The vehicle must have rocked up on its side...or something...I began to struggle/swim at a rate commensurate with my lung capacity...which at this point was zero... So I just kind of flapped my arms in a birdlike way...

The breath I took when I came to the surface should have burst both lungs...I immediately went to the floating position and tried to wrap my head around the whole "back from the dead" scene...

There on the bridge all of my buddies were lined up, cheering and slapping each other on the back like I had just scored the winning touchdown for the home team...Several vehicles were stopped...I couldn't hear anything...I was floating...floating...kind of letting the current move me.

When you hear the term "resting in the arms of Jesus"... that's exactly where I was...I knew it...He knew it,,.and I came to find out later that some of those guys on the bridge knew it...I swam to the bank on my own...unscathed but still really stuck in the " all I have to do is take a breath" mode...

I was carried up the bank in a sort of hero's welcome kind of way...The endless, exuberant chatter that comes with victory...in this case, surviving certain death...I was sent to the hospital and determined to be "indestructible" as was any good Infantry soldier...No one really asked about the experience. I wouldn't have told them anyway.

I sucked it up...the entire affair...because I knew that if I dwelt on it, I'd become one of those "testimonies" I'd heard in church so many times...and I'd have to deal with this Jesus issue once and for all...

To this day when I hear the hymn "Leaning on the everlasting arm"...I know what that actually feels like...I know...because I've been in those arms...rescued from the deep...swept up by the very hand of God...leaning in...latched onto...unable to finish by my own effort, capable only in his strength...and that is the safest most constant feeling there is...to know that, is the peace that comes with knowing him.

For a few years after that, I tried to ignore the truth of it...I took up residence on any barstool that would hold me...denying that God himself had rescued me from certain death...but I always knew... There just wasn't any other explanation.

There was no "lightning strike" conversion...as I had already genuinely submitted to God in my youth...There was however, a determination to look past it...which I understand to be normal in near death experiences...I just didn't want to deal with the only known reason for my survival...that being...the will of God. But there came a reckoning...It was a gradual acceptance...one that kept my attention...I don't remember the time or place but I finally surrendered all that is me...to all that is him...I accepted that only a merciful God could have snatched me out of that river...and he had a plan and a purpose for me...That was the "born again" experience for me. It was a long road but acceptance for some takes time. Thoughtful submission to an act of love is difficult for a warrior whose life is built on self-sufficiency.

Trusting God has a learning curve...I just wasn't good at that...For the longest time, I still felt that I could do it all on my own ...Even though I had accepted Christ, I hadn't really trusted him...That took dying to myself...Taking that breath under water every single day...Trusting that the hand would always be there to scoop me out…Invariably, it has been…I am thankful that the Lord decided to preserve my life that day. I am honored to serve him…He has my every breath…especially the last one.

I trust this short testimony helps you on your journey with the Lord. He is who he says he is…He loves you enough to die for you…and I can tell you personally that he will never leave you nor forsake you…especially when you are too weak to go it alone… That's when you can depend on him the most…

I'll end this in a place I remember as a child…It was an old flickering sign on the side of Ebenezer Baptist Church in Atlanta, Ga…I remember staring at it one night from the backseat of our car..I didn't really know what it meant then…but I can assure you that in my memory, it is the most important statement I ever read…

JESUS SAVES!

> *"Yea, though I walk through the valley of the shadow of death, I will fear no evil: for thou art with me; thy rod and thy staff they comfort me."*
> *-Psalm 23:4*

Unseen Hand

My first thought in the morning is to don a loin cloth and start applying the lake mud as camouflage. Then, I'll start gathering firewood and begin the process of making weapons of war, heating and bending cane and sharpening sticks for arrows, separating the poison plants from the good fruit bearing ones, collecting seeds and plants for medicines. I know instinctively what to do. I should hunt early. My mind wanders, sifting out the various ways to survive my enemies.

My instincts tell me to establish high ground, survey the surrounding area and observe the movement of animals as they forage. I am at home in the forest. I have skills taught to me by those who came before me.

I imagine the time is fast approaching when it will become necessary to teach the legions who will surely follow how to butcher and clean the animals. There is much to learn. They have little knowledge of how to survive. They know nothing of salting the meat for preservation or planting and tending the gardens that will feed them.

It will not be easy to lead an insurrection against this enemy, these lying dogs, these cowards who chose not to face us like men... these devouring barbarians who unleashed a weapon so fierce that we closed our doors to survive it.

We ignored the signs. We became comfortable in our shells. We will need much training. I don't know if there is time but I am not in charge of time. I am just another warrior taught to defeat my enemies in times like these.

In a moment of clarity, I have come to realize that those surviving the virus will soon be looking to their enemy for the cure. They aren't aware that the cure is the source of their sickness. They are the weak among us. We must survive them as well.

A slight cough that came outta' nowhere, reminds me that I should wash my hands and go back inside as there are people coming down the road...probably unaware of the real dangers they pose to me or that the pet they are walking will soon become their dinner.

I begin to accept that war just isn't what it used to be. My mind shifts to a more realistic view. Fighting an unseen enemy with weapons created to cause them fear and pain is of no value. Our bombs will only spread the disease. Our weapons will be used on each other to prevent any insurrection.

We must evolve as warriors. Our children's children are the new generals on the front lines...and there are no front lines. They war with microscopes in laboratories, facing untold reanimated versions of the curse that took us down. This is the new war. These are now the defenders of freedom...if they can muster the courage.

The cough is getting worse. Soon, I will need the services of the doctors but they will only treat the young. I have come to understand why. There just aren't enough resources to take care of the old. We, the once valiant protectors of liberty are, as we always suspected, defenseless and on our own. Liberty was just a passing fancy. It still amazes me how quickly we handed it over...and how naive we were to believe we possessed it like some carnival prize. We, the proverbial mighty...and how the mighty have fallen.

I ponder the thought of dying alone. The virus took my family long ago. I have survived this far by the grace of God and the genes of my forefathers granted me by the only friend I have left.

Still, I have need to fight. I am built for war. I sink to my knees and fight the battle the only way I have left...the only assurance of total victory. I ask God to grant us another day, another few minutes of worship, another meeting in His divine presence.

I ask only that His will be done. I am unworthy to ask anything more.

I delight in realizing that the old ways really are the best ways. I know the enemy much better now. He was unseen all along...as was the hand that will most certainly conquer him...the only One able to preserve any goodness that might remain among us...

As it is in heaven.

The Paperboy

I REMEMBER WHEN HE opened his shirt in front of the whole church. The audible gasp was almost performed in unison, as if a choir had been somehow summoned to sing it. The air left the room. He had come forward at the last moment, compelled to ask for prayer from the saints who had loved him from his youth and prayed him home from the war.

Every head suddenly faced forward, a rare event when church was almost over. Generally, it was a time when people were preparing to leave, standing for the final hymn, reaching for their bibles, gathering their coats ...but at that moment, the entire church was almost instantly still, all of us straining to hear his voice.

The sight of his scarred frame sent visible shudders through the congregation. Heads quickly hung. Intermittent, audible whimpers came from hearts so swollen; you could almost see them beating.

Some of the women looked away. The older veterans immediately dropped their heads in prayer. The kids shrieked a bit but they stared at the holes in his body, intrigued by the horrible image that stood before them. No one really knew the depth of his pain.

His wounds were massive. Five, maybe six raised mounds with deep, darkened pits in the middle, indented like craters, with discolored centers, the one in his shoulder the deepest, almost hollow...all of it hidden from plain view, discovered only when he chose to open his shirt.

We knew he'd been hobbled somewhat, just not to the degree we now could see. Some were entry wounds, other were exit wounds, as if the force of each one had turned him in different directions. I remember wondering how he could possibly stand.

I looked at my dad and saw the tears welling up in his eyes. That wasn't something my dad did. He didn't cry. I took notice and grabbed his hand, something I didn't do... He clenched it like it was forever. I'm sure he imagined me in this condition.

As we all gawked in an unsettling and intimate moment, he proceeded to describe how he'd received his wounds. His entire torso was bent from multiple surgeries. A couple of his rib bones had been removed, other bones wired together, the healed stitches crisscrossing like some ill-conceived railroad.

These weren't just battle scars. These were places where certain death had met a man on the field. The only reason he survived was the intercession of a mighty God who still had not fulfilled His purpose. I believe that day, in that moment, God revealed that purpose.

We had prayed for him while he was gone. We thanked God when he returned. Only now did we really understand the damage. Only now did we see the permanent scars that would be his to suffer for his entire life.

His eyes were sunken, hollowed from too many other battles beyond his obvious wounds...battles with sleep, sudden fear and depression. He spoke clearly over the sobs that followed. He was indeed desperate for prayer. He needed rest from the pain and misery. He was half the young man we remembered...but he was the biggest man in the room.

He stood as straight as he could. He pointed to his legs and explained how the bullets had shattered his hip and thigh. He described the pattern as a "Z" and that he had received automatic AK 47 fire across his body three times. It was literally a miracle that he stood at all. As he spoke, his father made a desperate, unsuccessful attempt to suppress his own pain. I remember specifically, the plea..."Dear God, help him!"

He'd been our paperboy before his "Senior trip" to Southeast Asia. He was ahead of me in school by a few years. His younger brother was in my class.

All he asked for was prayer for the pain. He didn't know how to survive it. He said he couldn't bring himself to take his own life after having been spared when others had not. It seemed he had begged enough for his own life and now he needed help from us.

I'd heard a lot of prayers go up in that small church. I'd knelt before God there, myself. But I'd never seen nor heard such an immediate heart felt, wide-open prayer. It went up like a rocket from men who had seen things in prior wars that no one should ever have to see.

It burst open the whole of heaven. My own soul churned with something I could only explain as a mixture of compassion, despair and sympathy. I had never experienced this degree of absolute worship before the God of the Ages.

Mothers spoke in the language of love for their own children. People who never publicly prayed spoke to God aloud, on their own. There was no single format or design. Some stood and grabbed the pew in front of them. Others fell to their knees, turning to put their heads in their hands pressing them against the hard-wooden seats. Hands lifted; every eye closed. Men prostrated themselves on the floor. The younger children grabbed their parent's hands and were quieted by a holy, reverent, spiritual reverberation. The echo itself humbled all of us.

The sobbing turned to wailing. The crescendo reaching clear up into heaven hanging like a cloud, at the very feet of Jesus, it seemed. It seared through every soul in the room, mine included. Our hearts literally broke for a man who had stood before other men and took the bullets intended for us. Words fail to describe the intensity of that prayer.

No one left unaffected. We all went down the aisle and tenderly hugged our friend and shook his hand. Not many words were exchanged. There just weren't any left. God Himself had inhaled them.

That's the day the paperboy brought the devastation of the war home to us. That's the day we all learned to pray. That's the day God chose to teach us all the spirit of prayer. That's the day I personally understood the difference in what it means to be in corporate prayer.

Slowly but surely, he recovered from his wounds, though he was never the same...but none of us ever recovered from the prayer. It somehow bound us in eternity. That was over fifty years ago... only yesterday, in eternity.

When he died some years later, the entire church turned out for his funeral. We all remembered the day the earth came out from under our feet and we spent a moment with our King, begging for help for this man who had indeed suffered for us. It was etched into our spirit. It bound us in heaven.

The paperboy had indeed delivered once again...as had our merciful and gracious God.

America needs to pray like that again. We've lost our edge because we no longer see the wounds it took to deliver us from evil. We no longer remember the sacrifice of Jesus. The scars in His hands and feet are a distant memory.

We kneel for the wrong reasons. We pray for the wrong things. We pledge allegiance to some form of godless morality that demands our loyalty. We are completely transparent, devoid of our once kindred hearts.

Only a powerful, righteous and just God can deliver us from the evil that has permeated our collective souls.

If you still love her, let your voice be heard above the foolish chatter of malcontents, self-indulgent protesters and prideful foolishness. Let your voice be heard in heaven!

Dear God, we beg you to once again bless this America. And once again, deliver us from evil.

> *Matthew 6:9-13*
> *Our Father who art in heaven, hallowed be thy name. Thy kingdom come. Thy will be done on*

earth as it is in heaven. Give us this day our daily bread, and forgive us our trespasses, as we forgive those who trespass against us, and lead us not into temptation, but deliver us from evil.

For thine is the kingdom and the power, and the glory, forever and ever.

Amen.

The Call

Angel: "Hello? You've reached Heaven.. How may I direct your call?"

Caller: "Yes, I'd like to make an appointment with Jesus..."

Angel: "Sure... Name please..."

Caller: "I kinda' need to speak with Him in a hurry. My names is Ike N. Waite and..."

Angel: "One moment Please...(brief interlude..." elevator musak)

Angel: "Mr. Waite? It says here you are recently deceased... Is that correct?"

Caller: "Well yes, That's kinda' the reason for the call... You see, I..."

Angel: "One moment please..."(More elevator musak... "Stairway to Heaven... You're kidding me, right?)

Angel: "Sir, Jesus isn't available..."

Caller: "What do you mean, He isn't available... I thought He was..."

Angel: "Omnipresent...He is... He doesn't take calls from your area code though..."

Caller: "What area code?... I'm dead... It's hot!... I'm gonna need to..."

Angel: "One moment please"(musak)

Angel: "Thank you for your patience, Mr. Waite..."

Calle: "Look... I'm kind of a big deal I wasn't supposed to..."

Angel: "Die?"

Caller: "Well yes... I had a lot going on... but if I could just talk to..."

Angel: Mr. Waite... "The way this works is, you died without ever having talked to Jesus... "

Caller: "I know, but I was busy and I gave a lot of money to the church and..."

Angel: "I'm sorry Mr. Waite... Jesus isn't available to you anymore..."

Caller: "But, I thought He was always available."

Angel: "He was... when you were alive... Many of our people tried to get you on board but you declined."

Caller: "This is crazy! I'm gonna need to talk to your Supervisor.."

Angel: "That would be Jesus, sir...and He isn't available, as I said... You'll have to take it up with Mister S."

Caller: "You don't mean Sata...

Angel: "We don't use his full name up here... Goodbye, Mr. Waite. Just a moment, I'll connect you... (Muzak: "Highway to Hell".... That's not right...)

Mr. S. : "Have a helluva' mornin'! ...Who are ya'... and whatchu' got for me?

Caller: "I was trying to speak to Jesus and mistakenly got transferred to you..."

Mr. S. :" They don't make mistakes up there, Ike..."

Caller: "How'd you know my name?"

Mr. S: "Ike... Buddy!... You're on my cellphone contacts list... Don't you remember that time you called me from Vegas?..."

Caller: "I was drunk...Surely you can't..."

Mr. S.: "How about all those calls from D.C, friend? ..."

Caller: "I needed the votes to..."

Mr. S. "How do you think you became a Congressman, Ike?"... Russians?... Bwahahahaha!... Welcome home, ol' friend. Good to have you!

Sure Footed.

I WATCH AND READ a lot of the commentary that passes for conversations in social media, particularly by those deemed important enough to deliver large doses of profundity to the weak-minded masses. I do it for a few reasons but mostly because it represents a microcosm of how society operates. By virtue of their fame or fortune, those who engage aggressively often expose the weaknesses of people in general and how quickly those followers align their own opinions with those they hold in high regard. Pardon my nonconformity.

I don't necessarily agree with opinions generated by self-proclaimed prophets or pseudo intellectuals. Neither do I live in fear of the conclusions reached by a consortium of media adept at bending the spoons of actual current events.

In fact, I don't live in fear about much at all. I've lived a long time with fear mongers. With that longevity comes an understanding that the world doesn't always move at the pace or direction I'd prefer but invariably it moves in the direction God intends, with or without our human permission.

From my perspective, I see an army of weaklings, lacking any discipline beyond blame and name-calling, using "social" media to announce their great wisdom, culled from whatever news has been preordained for consumption by the Omnipotent solicitors of Breaking News.

Invariably, the "enlightened" defer to some great expert (or some questionable article written by a self-appointed captain of morality) that proves their stance on any subject, particularly as it relates to the moral direction, we should all accept. I always wonder what moves people toward that particular light and how they come to accept corporate opinion as wisdom.

Therein lies the trappings of this all-consuming fire that leads us to a place of idolatry. In a moment's notice, we are able to gain access to all of human knowledge without the complexity of sound thinking or the observance of any source deemed spiritual or holy... because holiness is not the goal, God is not the answer and truth is subject to change. We conform to this idea because we are without foundation, or what I call "top down morality"...moral guidelines without any real foundation.

The prevailing thought seems to be that tolerance for others, no matter their version of truth or their reliance on their own conscience, is the chief end of man and equality the only foreseeable achievement.

That has never been the message of the bible. Never, ever…

What Christianity requires are absolute truths. We rely on the book God gave us and listen to the words, as they come directly from the only true source of wisdom. God Himself. We have turned it into a less than holy book because we no longer strive to be holy. We don't even know what that means much less include it when discussing our personal "lifestyles."

As Christians, we accept that Jesus is the Son of God and that He gave His life for us so that we would not suffer the consequences of our sin. He took that upon Himself. Believing that, we will share His wealth in eternity, in fact becoming co-heirs with Him.

We trust that God is who He says He is and that we are subject to His will above our own.

I see us faltering as the people of God, fearing retribution, literally feigning Christian behavior as if we are supposed to adapt to the rank and file observance of tradition and moral behavior, no longer anchored by the Master or Creator of our respective souls. I accept that as the prophetic "falling away" but I do not let it impede my attempts to be like Jesus and live for Him.

Our ability to answer the questions of life no longer exists beyond our own Christian circle of influence. We become more adept at conforming to the world rather than becoming steadfast in our relationship with our Creator and stepping out to tell others about Him.

It seemed the first thing to leave our churches is the one thing we need most...our prayer meetings. We no longer seek any sort of discipline in our prayer lives. We move solely on personal instinct and considered opinion...as if truth comes from celebrity and wisdom comes from corporate agreement.

We accept that the world is correct in their judgement of the book rather than to study the book itself. We set the book aside and read books about the book. We go to great lengths to explain the great doctrines of the bible in such detail, that faith in the supernatural has to align with "proven" science or irrefutable testimony from Christian leadership. We usurp the very power we claim, to be above any other.

We entertain the thought of other holy books being capable of giving us direction, as if God can't speak to us directly through

His word...or we claim that the work has been so corrupted in translation that it is hardly holy at all. That is the excuse many use to avoid the conviction brought about by studying God's word.

From my perspective (my claim being that wisdom comes from God and He alone is the only one to whom fear is justified) I see an army of self-righteous, weak, marooned typists, "opinionators" by trade if not by subjection... writing their own book from patched together articles that direct them toward a miserable condition... fearful, distraught, scurrying about, trying to push the world in the direction of their choosing, unaware that it will most certainly move in the direction of its sole Creator, foretold in the very book He provides.

Two words guide me when these irritating "malignats" seem to be buzzing all about...lighting on every word, irritants to those who seek truth and understanding amid fear and uncertainty.

The words "Fear Not" demand my attention. I have to ask, what should I fear from them? We each should ask, how is it that they make the world a better place given their propensity to resolve issues with complaint, and threat, insisting that we should all be more afraid than aware?

> *-2 Timothy 1:7-8*
> *"For God hath not given us the spirit of fear; but of power, and of love, and of a sound mind.*
> *Be not thou therefore ashamed of the testimony of our Lord, nor of me his prisoner: but be thou partaker of the afflictions of the gospel according to the power of God;"*

Insinuity

MANY MAY NOT necessarily agree with this...but then, we're not called to seek favor from other folks. I had a difficult time with this until I concluded that my opinion counts for nothing. But the truth stands on its own... eternally...so here goes...

Sometimes the insanity gets to me. I cannot accept, under any circumstances, that people are born morally conditioned to "do good" with a few stepping outside the lines sometimes doing bad things... This concept doesn't explain dropping children off of bridges or setting babies on fire... or beheading a fellow human for their nonconformance to some legalistic demand. Neither would it explain how an ideology steeped in hatred, (especially if deemed a religion) can evolve into a worldwide display of hatred and intolerance. No degree of "misstep" can explain how the murder of the unborn becomes acceptable in the sight of civilized people.

These are not instancing of bad behavior or mental illness or any other deviation from the "norm" These are displays of depravity... symptomatic of a greater evil...a controlled and violent causal force that overwhelms and destroys. ...evidences of the casualties of a war. Defined in real terms as "The battle between good and evil."

By any objective account, mankind is depraved...and spiraling at the speed of madness into the abyss of a literal hell. By any definition, hell is a place of eternal torment...a place of separation from God...a place where reconciliation with him is nonexistent.

We are each in need of a Savior...because we are each born into an evil environment (the world) ...subject to "the sin that so easily besets us," deceived for the most part by a power greater than ourselves. Evil exists...It lives in the absence of light...It grows and ferments in darkness. Evil has an administrator...a deceiver, one who "wanders about like a roaring lion, seeking whom he may devour." We are by virtue of our existence, subject to his "wiles." (schemes)

That is why Jesus came. That is why he died...because "God was in Christ" to reconcile a fallen people unto himself...and because without him, we continue on the path to destruction. By accepting him, we become one of his...no longer destined for separation from him, rather looking forward to an eternity spent with him.

> *-John 8:12*
> *"Then spoke Jesus again to them, saying, I am the light of the world: he that follows me shall not walk in darkness, but shall have the light of life."*

Rhetorical Mathology.

How many typists does it take to alter a fact?

How many inquiries into a false accusation equal the truth?

How many voices does it take to convert success to failure?

How many inquisitors are required to condemn the innocent?

How many poor, undocumented migrants equal an invasion?

How many petulant, rebellious children will it take to lead us to utopia?

How many sports "heroes" denouncing their country equal social justice?

How many malcontents equal a resistance?

How many edited and repeated reports equal propaganda?

How many celebrity awards equal relevant opinion?

How many passing deadlines will it take to cause settled science to become settled?

How much debauchery will it take to normalize perversion?

How many more must die to justify the deaths of millions of unborn?

How many adjustments are required to reverse what God has created?

How many books must be banned before we are completely enlightened?

How many statues must be removed before we erase our history?

How many bombs does it take to recognize a religion as peaceful?

How many children must be sold into sexual slavery before we are no longer accountable?

How much immorality must we tolerate before we exceed its limits?

When the math is done, and all the malcontents and self-involved peoples are sated, will the final product be a moral, productive, enlightened society?

According to this prophetic book, that answer is remarkably clear...

> *2 Timothy 3:1-5*
> *But understand this, that in the last days there will come times of difficulty. For people will be lovers of self, lovers of money, proud, arrogant, abusive, disobedient to their parents, ungrateful, unholy, heartless, unappeasable, slanderous, without self-control, brutal, not loving good, treacherous, reckless, swollen with conceit, lovers of pleasure rather than lovers of God, having the appearance of godliness, but denying its power. Avoid such people.*

Then Sings My Soul

THE SUN CREEPS up just beyond the end of the dock, casting orange flame across the morning sky. The water shimmers. In an instant, it changes from dark undulating waves to a shiny, sparkling sea, as if silver glitter were cast from some invisible cloud... It's coming...

"Oh Lord, my God"

I take a sip of coffee just to compose myself because I can see it developing right before my eyes. My wife is there beside me, silent and reverent as always. She too, enjoys the gift of daybreak. There's an unexplainable oneness in the moment, an excitement that builds with every glance toward the horizon. Taking it all in is impossible. All of nature is calm in the moment.

We anticipate what comes next. Of course, we've seen it before but each one is so new, so invigorating, so moving that we find ourselves leaning slightly forward in anticipation.

It is the spectacle of morning at our place on the lake. We are blessed to view another one. The sun inches up, then accelerates. It bursts on the scene with visual fanfare proclaiming the glory of the One who made this day...the One who made the very first day... and every day thereafter. The word "Rejoice" comes easily to mind and settles in the heart.

Suddenly, there it is in all its splendor. It is an unusually colorful, dare I say a spectacular morning...Orange and blue stripes set against a white, clouded background. The reds advance and cover the entire scene with bands of perfectly painted sky reflected in the water, mirroring the already magnificent view.

The colors begin to splash across the entire canvas as if it is set upon God's personal easel and we are allowed to peer over His shoulder to view the masterpiece. The brushstrokes are radical, determined, evidences of the artists hand. It is literally a display of such beauty that we put away any idea of capturing it beyond our own, limited memories. It is for us, a sacred, eternal event... an affirming gift of God for our mutual pleasure.

"When I in awesome wonder"

I hear a splash and I look to see a great blue heron devouring his catch. He moves gracefully across the bank, looking for another morsel. He stops to eye me from a distance, or maybe he's enjoying the sunrise as well... We sit motionless so as not to disturb him as he is somewhat skittish and we so enjoy observing his fishing expeditions.

I watch a bald eagle come out of nowhere, swoop down, legs forward, talons exposed, eyes on the target, literally snatching an unassuming mullet from just beyond the neighboring docks. As he returns to the nest, he announces his victory to the others. They reciprocate with their own piercing, congratulatory yelps. Breakfast in the treetops, is served.

A pileated woodpecker interrupts the scene, scrambling and chirping, then finding a branch on which to tap out his coded message...Its as if he is speaking the language of God to all creation. Perhaps I think too much...Perhaps I am caught up in the moment.

I ponder what science it must be that causes all of this remarkable beauty to happen with such regularity. I can't imagine that anyone could accept as simply "natural" what is clearly a recurring, supernatural, miracle.

I reach for my Bible and open it to my study. I thank Almighty God for the moment and read a passage from the Psalms as is my custom.

> "Consider all, the world Thy hands have made..."

I begin to wonder what the unbelieving scientist sings...I wonder what fills the atheist's heart. I wonder if there are songs for the agnostic, the cynic, the doubter. To what do they attribute this daily miracle...this burst of morning and the accelerated movement in all of nature that speaks directly to the evidence of the Creator they unknowingly seek? Surely, they are grateful for these moments. To whom is their gratitude directed? To what does their soul sing?

I cannot fathom the motivation of those who attribute this beauty to anything generated by natural means, as if the gift comes because it must...as if their benefactor simply rewards them for their presence in His creation...because He must...

Indeed, How Great Thou Art... that You would reward us with such splendor!

> *Job 12: 7-10*
> *"But ask the animals, and they will teach you, or the birds in the sky, and they will tell you; or speak to the earth, and it will teach you, or let the fish*

in the sea inform you. Which of all these does not know that the hand of the LORD has done this? In his hand is the life of every creature and the breath of all mankind."

Woman of Mass Destruction

YOU CAN SMELL fear in the air as she approaches, her steps measured and brisk. She is focused on the horizon, sure footed and stealthy beyond the normal abilities of most ninja warriors. She has an inherent, tried and tested will.

The others can't help but snicker at her oafish assistant as he lumbers behind her carrying the high-grade ammunition. He too has a weapon of considerable potential. There is something sad about his inability to wield it with any consistency.

The super blood wolf moon is behind her now. It is the day after. She breathes in the cool air and slips on the fingerless gloves that will allow her to feel the death that will come by her hand. She is one with the violence that is about to unfold.

The enemy knows that death is imminent. She uncases her weapon and spins the cylinder... They hear the clicks and shudder. It's too late to move away from the onslaught. Death is at the very foot of their beds.

She loads the weapon skillfully, without wasted movement. She picks and chooses from the ammunition box that holds the various propelling primers, floating devices, cartridges and multi gaged wire.

She launches her assault with the accuracy of a practiced archer. This won't take long... They can't resist the power of the pheromone dripping from her fingers. Certain destruction permeates the very air around her. Their fate is sealed.

THWACK! There are no screams yet the sound is deafening...a perfect strike, as usual... the violent convulsions of her natural enemy cause her face to contort in a detectable, almost sardonic grin.

Her assistant nods with approval, smiles and says something under his breath in a language known only to fallen angels and those in the nether regions. He must fake his response or he will not learn of her many skills. It is a wonder to behold despite his aversion to her much heralded abilities.

Again, and again she loads and launches. Surely, she can't keep this pace... The slaughter continues for hours until her murderous urges are sated. He watches with respect...and learns...

She is mighty Lynn, Fishtress of the Lake... Owner of the dock... Queen of all she surveys...Wife of Poseidon...Keeper of the Trident of Neptune...

It is painful fishing with this Grim Reaper! What is even worse. she cleans and cooks them so I am left to the simple task of watching and learning...and sucking up. It's no longer even a contest. She has the patience of Job and the skill of an ancient ninja warrior.

She is indeed the Fish Whisperer and I her trusted and fishless sidekick.

Euphemasia.

IT'S BECOME NEARLY impossible for me to watch a newscast, if it can even be called that anymore. I've become more of an observer than an interested party. Not that I've suddenly arrived but I find myself more attuned to the overall deception than the actual news.

Politics doesn't really interest me as much as it once did, as I've discovered no common ground is attainable, or even intended between the parties. So, each version of news must be viewed from the position of its own bias. How is that even healthy?

That said, I'm fascinated by the subtle shaping of words and phrases that completely change the landscape of any news item. It's how the game is played, polishing words until their intent and meaning are altered beyond the scope of their original definition, abrading the sharp edges of language until an otherwise contemptible act becomes nothing more than an acceptable rite of passage.

"We all do it"…Even the Bible says that…So sin, for instance (and for lack of a better word) must be viewed as socially acceptable… particularly sexual sin because that is widely held as acceptable behavior unless the other side has been found out, at which point it becomes a deplorable act. I haven't really figured that sexual blame game out yet. For the most part though, diminishing sin requires repetitive dismissal or it remains sin and of course, we simply can't allow the word sin to be allowed in polite (now politically correct) society.

So, we must weave these antiquated ideas (like sin) into something more presentable to the masses so that folks aren't offended... or heaven forbid "guilted" into anything so preposterous as confession of sin or (gasp) repentance

Without sin, God is diminished because He is the only one who can forgive actual sin... So, we cannot utter words like "sin" or "God" because they are inextricably bound. That much is actually true. Jesus still saves. He died for our sins.

By removing accountability, we denounce even His existence because without God, we can only sin against ourselves and our own acts of forgiveness are enough. The effort is to show that humanity is quite capable of atoning for our own sin without that ugly depiction of Jesus doing it for us on that horrible, bloodied cross. From that perspective, there are no sins against God... There are only missteps and tragic circumstances brought about by "unknown" forces.

We've come to a place where God is the name that is most unspeakable in any form. God the Father, God the Son and God the Holy Spirit are all names we shouldn't utter as they tend to cause conflict, and of course, we can't have conflict not authorized by the news agencies or the state (as if there were a difference) ...We just can't have these zealots "contending for the faith." It's offensive.

Our own worldly lusts are viewed as nothing more than natural, human responses to natural, normal stimuli. The language must of course, follow or consequences could be blamed on our own choices...and since there is no sin. there can be no evil. Thus, there is no God. Indeed, the nail has become the hammer.

The taking of unborn lives has become a matter of "personal choice." Deviant behavior becomes "lifestyle." Conviction becomes "conscience." religion becomes "fanaticism." Even "truth" is subjective and of course all we need to do is "identify" and we can change our very DNA. These are just a few alterations we've come to accept.

We are susceptible to these who weave their messages from whole cloth because we have changed masters. We seek societal direction rather than Godly wisdom. We accept the definitions of social engineers who constantly weave the words into acceptable language rather than to look to the Scriptures for direction.

The wages of sin haven't changed...nor has the director of it turned over a new leaf. He and his henchmen have only muted the original version and made the trip to a destructive end more comfortable...

Jesus, is still the name above every other name...even if it's only whispered. One of these days though, the only language that's going to matter is what we say from bended knee...even then we are each "without excuse."

> *2 Peter 2:2,3*
> *And many will follow their sensuality, and because of them the way of truth will be blasphemed. And in their greed, they will exploit you with false words. Their condemnation from long ago is not idle, and their destruction is not asleep*

Truth Extraction

A SIMPLE OBSERVATION THAT points to the ruination of what used to be America, is the attachment of "wings" that float the idea of separation...I'd venture to say that all "biblical" truth is now considered "right wing speak" believed only by those who accept the bible itself as containing any truth.

Relegating truth to any political faction is a deceptive means of suffocating it. The truth can't "set you free" if it is assigned a space and told to sit there. The truth can't "march on" with one leg... Truth is the source of freedom. It is the source of justice. It is constant and immutable. Ideals grounded in truth are indeed the path by which we progress toward a righteous end.

The truth is rarely expressed by those who keep secrets or promote political agendas. It needs to be searched out and sorted from the information heap. That isn't accomplished by "unnamed sources"...or "sources close to the investigation." These are catch phrases used to indicate a kink in the truth chain. There has to be an original truth, otherwise, we seek nothing. We move toward nothing. In essence, we achieve nothing.

We need ageless wisdom to discern truth. We need a source for it...not a rendition of it. Truth needs to be distinguished above all else if we are to advance as a people.

There doesn't seem to be many who agree anymore, without a common source, we continue to be divided. Division provides enough distortion to create doubt...and doubt is the artillery that creates mass confusion.

Knowing that Jesus claimed to be the way, the truth and the life should make us all interested enough to seek Him out...to discover whether His claims are factual...to do as He says so that we may individually and corporately achieve the results He promises...

Because He is the truth, we can believe this..."and you shall know the truth, and the truth shall set you free." There is no freedom without truth. Truth is not political. Truth is not an ideology. Truth stands alone as the only measure of goodness when evil announces its presence.

> *-Psalm 86:11*
> *"Teach me your way, O Lord, and I will walk in your truth; give me an undivided heart, that I may fear your name."*

Collateral Effects.

I LISTEN MORE INTENTLY to the anthem. I sing louder! I know every word and the history behind them. I no longer just mouth the words. I belt each word out loud enough to embarrass those that don't!

I stand quickly when I know it is about to be played. I stand at the "proper" position of attention. I put down whatever is in my hand and I stop the chatter...sometimes in mid-sentence. I announce that they are about to play the Star-Spangled banner and I become an example! I put my hand over my heart and I press it down hard enough to feel my own American blood pulsing through my veins.

I keep my eyes glued to that flag because that is the focus. That is what this America is all about. Everything else is a distraction. That banner represents the greatest country that ever existed. We don't call her "Old Glory" for nothing. We are indeed blessed to be here. I swell with pride at the sight of her and the words of the anthem. It is the moment I choose to rightfully engage her detractors!

I fight back tears as I remember my family and friends and their sacrifice...I sometimes have to gasp for breath as I think about all those who have given everything so that I can be a part of this celebration... this anthem... this testimony to a loving God who blessed this ground and those who gave themselves for her.

I don't see or hear protests because in America, malcontents are allowed to breathe the same air. I've learned to accept the ignorant. They don't realize the ground they stand on has been earned and that the places they drop their knees have been gifted by a mighty God! They don't understand that they disgrace themselves. Who could possibly explain it to them?

I know America has enemies. They mark their own spots. They point to themselves as though they are proud of their display. They have no idea how many simply shake their heads at their lack of any semblance of dignity. They believe that respect is earned by winning a game and that glory somehow keeps score. They have no idea that American blood is thicker than Gatorade…

They call me "nationalist" and a few other choice words…because someone told them once that loving your country is a bad thing and that patriotism is no longer cool…Honoring our fallen was never meant to be…but it seems that many don't understand honor. They don't understand the meaning of the word because they have none of their own. It was never incumbent on them to earn any.

I don't flinch during the anthem because Americans don't…They never have! My father and his entire generation stood tall against those who hated that flag! They carried it through jungles and mountains, in the air and across the seas. They stuck it in mud and hammered it in ice and saluted it every day because it represented their home…their family their honor. They've folded and handed it to wives and mothers in thousands of courts where courage and valor are truly decided. Yet still, there are those who can't make the distinction.

Our kids and grandkids are still fighting for that flag every single day, all over the world. Without their sacrifice there would be no game. Without their dedicated service there would be no flag and without their blood, there would be no America to protest…

There!

THE WHOLE PLACE smelled like cake. I found that exhilarating... but I had more to think about than the pleasant smells...It was Judgement Day...and I was next!

"Step this way...Jesus will be with you in a moment," said the kindly old gentleman as he hooked the latched, velvet rope behind me.

I moved past the cordoned area and stepped in front of the throne...I couldn't see Him yet but I could sense He was there. Everything was crystal clear...not foggy or cloudy like in the movies. Nothing here was like any movie. It was bright and clear.

Then suddenly, without fanfare, because clearly, He needed no introduction, there He was...Jesus! ...The Christ! ...Almighty God in the flesh.

I approached, anxious to meet Him. He spoke my name. It was somewhat calming that He knew my name and that I recognized His voice. I wanted to tell Him so much but I just stood there, unable to speak, intensely aware that I was standing in the presence of Holy God. Humility and reverence overtook me.

My knees gave way. In an instant every transgression, every lie, every unfaithful act I'd ever committed against Him overwhelmed my thoughts. All the questions I dreamed of asking had turned to grief. My heart was burdened with the realization that all of this was about to happen, just as I'd read... just as I'd heard... just as I'd believed...

I knew the options. I believed in the outcome. Still, there was the burden of not having always been faithful, of unrepented transgression, of failed relationships, of my own vanity...all of it welling up inside my head, gripping my soul.

It was then that my sins weighed more than I could bear. I continued to kneel before Him, sobbing, trying to express what I couldn't even ask...I knew exactly what I deserved. I was without excuse. Any response would have been foolishness.

I tried not to look at Him but curiosity overwhelmed me. I didn't stare but I wanted to see His face. His gaze connected with mine. His eyes were gentle. His voice controlled, not stern or demanding...but calm and inviting. He didn't shout, though His voice rolled through the hall like approaching thunder. He did not appear to be angry with me or anyone. He was, in His very person, just and merciful in the same moment.

I looked back down at the golden floor my head bowed in shame.

"I don't know what to say. I could have done so much more in Your name." I muttered. My statement fell short of its intended, penitent goal.

"Tell me you love me!"

"You know I do, Lord. I'm nothing without You!"

Then, in what I could only describe as a heavenly instant, He simply said, "You are forgiven." He held out His hands as if to wave me closer. I saw the scars...I trembled at the thought of what happened on that cross...I felt more deeply than I ever had...I continued to sob, partly from the shame and partly from mounting gratitude.

In that moment, I knew what He'd done for me. I'd accepted it long ago but seeing His nail scarred hands was all the evidence I'd ever need, if I could ever fully understand ever. I'd always believed, but in that moment, I understood...He died for me! I was bought for a price.

I put my face to the floor. There was no other way to thank Him... no other way to say I'm sorry...no other way to show Him the honor and glory He deserved. My whole being was shaken beyond anything I'd ever experienced.

I could not stand. It just wasn't possible...and then He said it...Just as I had always believed He would.

"Well done, my good and faithful servant." Then, He reached out and wiped away my tears...just...like...that! His touch indescribable...His love beyond anything I'd ever encountered.

My next breath was an affirmation as I breathed the air of heaven. My home...I was home!

My heart nearly burst with gratitude knowing full well that He alone had done all the work, that He alone had made the sacrifice for all of my transgressions. That's when I knew what the words "He alone is worthy." really meant.

Suddenly, there was no more sorrow...no sadness...no pain... Forgiveness forever. I would experience this forever. I had no idea what eternity was but I knew I was there.

I looked around the Great Hall and started to make out silhouettes of others. I could see down to the earth and up into the entrance to the mansions above. One of them had my name inscribed just above the entrance, as if Jesus Himself had written it...because He had.

I noticed that no one was standing...Every knee was bowed. Every being above and below came into focus in the place called eternity.

Then, like a great chorus, we all uttered the same words as if directed in our very souls do so,

"Jesus Christ is Lord!"

> *Philippians 2:10 &11*
> *...that at the name of Jesus every knee should bow, of those in heaven, and of those on earth, and of those under the earth, and that every tongue should confess that Jesus Christ is Lord, to the glory of God the Father.*
>
> *Isaiah 25:8*
> *He will swallow up death forever. The Sovereign LORD will wipe away the tears from all faces; he will remove his people's disgrace from all the earth. The LORD has spoken.*

Gentle On My Mind.

I REALLY COULDN'T TELL you why I came out of the skid... I'm certain though, that it was some big heart somewhere, probably my dad's, maybe a sweet lady who heard his plea in a church room, maybe even a prayer group somewhere that made the connection... but I do know that God, in His awesome grace and mercy, bent his ear toward that prayer and nodded in my direction...Nothing else could have generated the power to stop my nosedive. I was determined to be the last man standing, even if it was standing in the fire. Ask anyone who knew me back in the day!

There can be no single reason for it. I wasn't particularly close to God. I of course, appealed to Him when I'd get into trouble or wake up with the shakes in some room I didn't remember entering. The tremors were pretty bad sometimes...bad enough to where I would drink only half cups of coffee... Otherwise I'd spill it all over my trembling hand and scald myself.

The hangovers were miserable as well and depending on the chemical mixture, I could generally tell what type of drug I had taken and whether or not I would be able to navigate my way home... wherever that was. It was a pretty cumbersome existence...but I got through it. I had no fear of the end. I just figured it would be abrupt...I had lost any desire to reconfigure the mess that was me.

There was divorce and pain and drama to last a lifetime but somehow, the bullet stopped before it passed through anything vital. There was no epiphany, no disaster, no incurable disease... there was just a moment in time when I knew that I'd had enough. It all ended in a genuine desire to just do better. It was like the end of a bungee jump when you suddenly snap back into a place that makes sense...

I'd been to the meetings and heard the stories a thousand times...I went to anything that looked like a place to stay out of trouble. I moved all over the country trying to rehab from all the rehab and I finally landed in a place that is still comfortable... still gentle, calming, still motionless in a turbulent world...still easy... still, still...

I don't know for sure who's prayer God heard but I'm sure that if it was mine, it needed some heavy interpretation. I probably muttered it from a barstool just before I decided to join the others in a game of "Name That Pharmaceutical."

The point is this. God hears your prayer even when you don't have the good sense to pray it. He deals with your heart...your soul... your innermost being... He can see into the depths of your pain and pull you out of whatever hell you're in... because He's God... and He loves you. Write that part down for future reference.

If He can yank me out of the fire, you have to believe that He's going to be there for you. Just ask Him... and know this too... Pray for your kids. I'm certain that my dad was praying for me no matter where I was in the world...in whatever condition...I'll get a chance to thank him for that one of these days...because he intervened on my behalf and spoke to the only one who can enter a heart and answer those prayers. Nothing else makes any sense at all.

It's Jesus, friends. Nothing else offers hope or a future... No one else can take the load...or stop the train...He's God, ya' know... He's everything He says He is.

> *Matthew 11:28-29*
> *Come unto me, all ye that labor and are heavy laden, and I will give you rest. Take my yoke upon you, and learn of me; for I am meek and lowly in heart: and ye shall find rest unto your souls*

That Moment...

GOD INTERESTS ME...I'M not sure why He doesn't interest everyone but apparently, not many folks seek Him out anymore. I can't imagine why not. I've always found him to be welcoming and acceptant of whatever burden I might lay at His feet. I read His word each time with renewed interest because I know my answers are there. I don't know why so many people refuse to look for some break in the storm. That's not mine to understand, I guess... but to me, there is no greater source of comfort than to read the inspired word of God. That's what it is actually... and I've come to know it as just that.

I've learned not to tackle it. It's God's word, meant to confront, convict and conform me. It's not a "book of rules" though many exist... or a "condemnation of mankind" though many are. It's a perfect explanation of what God wants me to be...and who He wants me to know. The Bible is the revealing of Jesus Christ. The measure of His word is beyond my own ability to comprehend so I must wait for God to speak to me through it. That's how it works. It is as if the very words touch me and I understand what I didn't before...a bit like solving an intense math problem only without all the math, if you will...

I'm burdened with the world. It overwhelms me most of the time. I couldn't possibly deliver myself from all the snares meant to entangle me... It's a difficult place, with sharp turns and jagged edges... Always some kind of trouble brewing, sometimes at every turn it seems...treacherous consequences, evil people, dangerous pitfalls... Sometimes, I can actually see the whole thing imploding around me...It makes me uncomfortable to live here...perhaps because I know I'm just visiting or perhaps it's God trying to get my attention...making me understand what part I play in His plan.

That's when I look up... only because I like the uncluttered view up there... because I know God is all around me. That's when the uncertainty disappears...That's when the words I've read fall into place. That's when the size of me comes to grips with the significance of Him. There's a reason we use the word Almighty in reference to God.

Then there's the epiphany...the moment I accept that He's a big God, and I'm important enough to Him that He gives me a listen... makes me a path... calms my soul... loves me beyond my own capacity to love Him back...provides His direction... creates in me a greater vision... removes my doubt...erases my fear... deals with my demons...forgives my greatest sins... That's when I understand that He makes me entirely... His!

> *Romans 8:30-32*
> *What then shall we say in response to these things? If God is for us, who can be against us? He who did not spare His own Son but gave Him up for us all, how will He not also, along with Him, freely give us all things?*

A Matter of Choice.

TODAY I AM choosing to be victorious over all that works against me. I am choosing to circumvent those who would seek to obstruct my view...I am choosing life over existence, happiness over sadness and victory over victim hood. I am trusting Almighty God to assist me in all that I do because without him I accomplish nothing of eternal value.

I am choosing to live life because the alternative is complaint and misery. I am choosing success over failure because all things are possible through Christ who strengthens me. I am choosing to be deliberate in my thinking and conscious of the goodness that surrounds me...Despite the presence of evil. I am choosing to do good.

I am entering this day prayerfully with a vision greater than myself. There are things to learn...people to meet...new sights, smells, sounds... all of the richness of life...given me by the Creator of all that is good.

Where there is suffering, I will serve with joy... Where there is hatred, I will offer love. Where there is confusion, I will attempt to bring order. Where there is hopelessness...I will point to the hope that lies within me. Today, I will enjoy my service to the Lord. Today is the day He has given.

I choose to view today in color...because the Lord is with me.

> *Job 34:4*
> *"Let us discern for ourselves what is right; let us learn together what is good."*

Jogging Around the Mental Block.

MY DAD, WHEN he was 85 years old, would point to his heart and say, "They still haven't made a pump that will last 85 years... and this one is still pumping."... In his mind, that was enough affirmation of the miracle that is the human body...Nothing else beyond that exemplified the wondrous nature of how precisely we humans are built. Each time he would have a surgical procedure, he would announce how long that particular original component had lasted.

Since having my hip replaced, I've started to think in the same terms. I remember all the rigors I put my own body through and am constantly amazed that it still works exceptionally well considering the punishment I heaped upon it. I am truly blessed in that regard.

I had concluded however, that I probably would never run again due to my age, the additional weight I had gained since the surgery and the new mechanical joint. It just made sense to enjoy a sedentary lifestyle and not get overly involved in speeds beyond my capacity. Still, I began to walk and exercise. A couple of setbacks, (i.e. nerve issues and a bout with bursitis) caused me to slow my pace...but I recovered with nothing more than a slight limp and limited distance that gets longer each day.

A few days ago, I was watching my neighbor spread rock on my driveway with his tractor. I suddenly found myself a bit in the way and impulsively jogged a short distance in the opposite direction. I didn't even think about it at the time... but it did surprise me a little once I realized what I'd done. I started to understand that I had limited myself by thinking in terms of my injury instead of in terms of my recovery. I had put limits on my own condition. I actually could run if I had to, which meant that I could recover completely, given time.

I still have the limp and I still have limited endurance when it comes to distance. There are actual physical limitations that I have to accept... but what there is not, is a limit to what I can and can't do. I'm not exactly sure how the human will works or how long it lasts but it appears as though I needed a replacement...I am beyond thankful that God has performed that surgery and that I can once again look forward to the productive use of my legs beyond what I had hoped.

Since I've learned to "scoot" out of the way, I will now concentrate on "skedattling" and maybe even a little "galavantin'" ...just to make my mama proud!

At least now I know not to create boundaries and put myself in charge of my ultimate condition. I am aware of the one who does the healing... and there ain't no half way.

> *Psalm 139:14*
> *"I praise you because I am fearfully and wonderfully made; your works are wonderful; I know that full well."*

The Best Day of Dr. Billy Graham's Life.

"SOMEDAY YOU WILL read or hear that Billy Graham is dead. Don't you believe a word of it. I shall be more alive than I am now. I will just have changed my address. I will have gone into the presence of God." ~ Billy Graham

My dad would always tell us when there was a Billy Graham Crusade on T. V. We awaited them with much anticipation because my dad loved to hear him speak. He was a devout Christian and would explain to us how God was using Billy Graham to reach the world. We didn't understand all of that. We were just kids and it seemed to us like just another night in church... but I do remember listening intently to what he had to say. Even as a child I would mull over the message and look things up in my Bible. I wasn't sure what I believed about all that but it caused me to think about eternity.

It wasn't until I was twelve years old that it all came together for me. It was a long night and I couldn't sleep. I was wrestling with something, maybe a child's guilt over some minor offense or a problem at school. Still, there was a disturbance beyond normal childish burdens. So, I began to pray. I asked Jesus to help me with whatever it was.

After tossing and turning for a while, I literally felt a calm that I had never experienced. It was as if a hand had touched me and all the worry and anxiety just disappeared. All of the times I had heard the message came together and I knew... I just knew, that the Lord was with me. I remember the comforting thought that it was an eternal matter and that I had dealt with Almighty God on the subject of my "personal forever."

I ran downstairs to talk to my dad. I really didn't want to wake him but when I did, he wasn't as disturbed as I thought he would be. He asked me a few questions and smiled as I answered them. My mother listened intently to my responses.

The next day I had a meeting with our Pastor, Dr. John Manous. He was a loud country preacher and he knew his Bible. He walked me through what was then called the Roman road... passages that led us to a "right relationship with Jesus Christ." We talked about the event for what must have been a couple of hours. He was satisfied that my encounter was real and that I was "saved" as far as all of our understanding of salvation and what that meant in eternity.

I didn't quite understand it all but I did know this. Jesus loved me and I would forever be sheltered in His arms because of what He did on the cross. He took my sins upon Himself and He died so that I might live with Him in heaven when my time here is through. There is no greater love than that. Believing that, I was baptized the following Sunday. I didn't always live it...but I knew it. That was the confidence I had.

So "Thank You" isn't enough for Dr. Billy Graham... not for one who planted that seed in me and millions of others... A life lived beyond his own, reaching out to others, preaching and teaching so that they too might experience eternal life... and "Rest in Peace" seems odd to say because I imagine that Jesus is keeping him pretty busy (and vice versa answering all of his questions.) I imagine him shaking hands with the many people that are there because Billy Graham introduced them to Jesus.

Can you just imagine Billy Graham meeting Matthew, Mark, Luke and John... and all the old prophets...and Mary and Ruth and... countless others? ...Heaven is rejoicing right now and you can bet a dollar to a Carolina barbecue sandwich, that Billy Graham is too!

He's checking out his new body. That's got to be fun after living so many years in one that was failing. I'm sure my dad and he have finally met face to face. I can't say it for a fact but I can imagine my dad looking Billy Graham square in the eye and saying,

"Race ya'!"

> *John 3:16*
> *"For God so loved the world that he gave his one and only Son, that whoever believes in him shall not perish but have eternal life."*

Just Listen

GLOBALLY, 250,000 PEOPLE die each day. Christians believe that each of them spends eternity in one of two places. It is our hope...and our greatest challenge...to point others in the direction of Jesus Christ. He said of himself, "I am the way, the truth, and the life. No one comes to the Father but by me." There is nothing to "interpret" in that statement, it is either absolutely true...or absolutely false...and that is the decision each of us has to make... whether or not Jesus is who He says he is...or He is not!

As Christians, we understand the magnitude of that decision. Our intention is not to "force anything down your throat"...rather it is to introduce you to the one, true, living God who offers you a reservation in heaven, through his son, Jesus.

You see, we believe that every person is an opportunity. You are important enough to us that we want to share the message of Jesus. In short, we'd like to know you forever! We'd like to have you as an eternal friend, not just a casual acquaintance... How can that be considered anything but love?

Listen to your Christian friend when he or she extends their hand. To them, it is an expression of love and a desire to share eternity with you by introducing you to the one who died so that you might live!

If we come off a little too bold, consider it the enthusiasm God has for you, to make you one of his own. He has proven to us his capable and loving nature. Sharing that with you is not an insult.

It is an attempt to include you in the love and power we have experienced.

Our instructions are clear.

> *Matthew 28:18-20*
> *And Jesus came and said to them, "All authority in heaven and on earth has been given to me. Go therefore and make disciples of all nations, baptizing them in the name of the Father and of the Son and of the Holy Spirit, teaching them to observe all that I have commanded you. And behold, I am with you always, to the end of the age."*

Truth Is.

I COULD SPIN WORDS if I wanted... It's not hard to tweak the truth... But believing as I do, I don't think that's what God has in mind for me...

Here's what I believe. Indulge me for a paragraph or two as I walk through this with you. I'm built for this kind of thing but certainly not one of the high and mighty. I am probably more like you than you wish to believe but on the grand scale of humanity, we think and talk and act in a consistent way. We all transgress against God. That is the great equalizer.

I believe beyond a shadow of a doubt, that God exists. I see Him in virtually everything. I haven't always but in seeking to learn about Him, my faith has been strengthened beyond our initial encounter because I've searched diligently for answers and reasoned with God. I continue to study His ways and listen to His words. That in and of itself, is evidence of a very clear, very concise biblical message. "Seek and you will find." It's a simple reality.

Discovering that we are all actually transgressors against God is a difficult but necessary truth. Once we accept that, we realize that nothing we do can reconcile us with God. We are in fact, born into that condition ...separated from God...

I believe, because God loved me so much, He sent His Son Jesus, to be the propitiation, the atoning sacrifice, for my Sins. I believe He was sinless and crucified in order to reconcile me with Himself. I believe he was buried in a tomb and three days later he walked out of that tomb...I believe He conquered death because He was and is now, who He says He is...the Son of God, God in the flesh... I believe that as a result of His work on the cross and my faith in Him, that I will someday meet Jesus face to face, in a place called heaven...because this Jesus is the physical manifestation of a triune and holy God. He lives in heaven and has prepared a place for me in eternity... and I believe that to be the literal, gospel truth as stated in the Bible. I believe the Bible is the inerrant, infallible and inspired word of God, so not much wiggle room there...

I believe that we can each establish a relationship with that very same Jesus because He asks us to do so. I believe as you read this, Jesus is aware that you are being presented with the truth of the gospel. It is by His leading that it is written. Yours is to respond to that message and accept or deny it...or seek further information...not because I say you should, rather because God says that you should seek Him. ("Draw near to God and He will draw near to you."–James 4:8)

This has nothing to do with argument. It's a personal testimony of what I believe and why I believe it. Such is the way of messengers.

I also understand that many do not accept or believe any of that. My job is to use what God has given me to present that message to you, whoever you might be... because you're the one reading this. You see, God controls the message and the hearts of those to whom it is presented. It's His world... We're just living in it.

The fact that you don't believe these things doesn't make us enemies. It doesn't even put us at odds on a human level. We can both still feed the hungry and assist the poor and help our neighbors out when they need us. We can still love and laugh and enjoy each other's company. That doesn't change.

My belief is that we are each presented with the evidence and can accept or deny what is put before us. That requires a look at the consequences of rejecting that information. In reality, I can't change how you feel or think about the universe or the Creator of it...All I can do is live a life that serves the purpose for which I believe I was created.

It's those consequences that are the problem for believers. We don't want you to suffer separation from God just because you've never really been properly introduced. We don't want to "thump" you with our bibles or berate you because you don't believe what we believe. That's not how we operate, nor should it be...We bring a message of love, from a position of love about the Creator, who is love... If we don't, we're not following the instructions.

In a lot of ways, we feel responsible because we fail too. God's purposes are served when we tell the story... however we do that. Many of us feel that a sense of urgency is required due to the times in which we live... Still, the idea is to love you and expose that love as genuine. So, our hearts break when you reject the entirety of our message.

It doesn't make you any less "spiritual" because you don't believe these things to be possible or even plausible, any more than it makes us more holy... It just means that we have investigated and accepted the evidence as it was presented. We have taken a step of faith and proceeded to further our investigation.

We want you to investigate as well because we have found peace in Jesus and wisdom in His word as a result of our inquiry. We want that for you. That is the love that we have for you. It comes from above. Our hope is that you won't misinterpret that effort.

I think the best way to put it is this... With any great discovery, there is a moment of glaring disbelief...I'm sure people asked, could we REALLY go to the moon? cure a disease? transplant a heart? or bring water to the desert? Could we actually communicate with others with a handheld device? These questions were unanswerable until they literally pulled back the curtain and peered into the possibilities...That's when they proceeded to follow the path to discovery... Ask the right questions... Remove the obstacles... Discover the possibilities.

Those things were impossible at one time. They couldn't be believed because there was no conceivable way to make them happen...So, in order to make them happen, someone somewhere, needed a little faith... faith in technology, faith in the ability of people to solve problems, faith in innovation and faith in the, dare I say "unseen." Someone took that faith to the next level and went about the business of making it a reality. Someone believed that the sky wasn't the limit and accepted the possibility that what we thought we knew we didn't fully know.

We have to view faith for what it is... It's not just the belief in a higher power or a grand designer or an "eye in the sky. " It is the belief, indeed a hope, that there is something or someone that guides the universe and humanity specifically. Faith is the effort beyond the questioning. Faith is a direction. Faith is putting feet to our belief. There is a way to grow one's faith. It comes by intentionally feeding it from the word of God (Romans 10:17 "So then faith comes by hearing, and hearing by the word of God.")

We each have to place our faith in something... Why not a God who loves us? ... one who created us, walks with us, guides us and knows us intimately? Ask yourself why you would reject the possibility of a living, loving God...Then ask Him.

Consider this.

> *Hebrews 11:1*
> *Now faith is the substance of things hoped for, the evidence of things not seen.*

Bibleonians

MY DAD WAS a bible teacher and "contextualist" He was not necessarily a literalist, (as the word is misused) though he would state that every word of the bible is true...He understood the need for the "whole counsel" of God beyond the exercise of casual reading. He was in fact, "Berean" in his study of the Word of God and took his gift of teaching very seriously.

He used to say that the New Testament was a template that could be placed over the Old Testament and truth would emerge from that process.

I too believe that, though I am not near the student he became...I can only aspire to that level of study and unless God gifts it, I could never attain his level of wisdom. I was blessed with him. He engaged me like no other can. I grew to understand him and wish I'd had more time for Q and A sessions. He welcomed my questions and always "discipled" me when I sought answers.

Now that he has been with the Lord for about 3 years, I still miss just picking up the phone and asking him a question and getting a solid answer. That was my preferred method of study as I could trust that he would never steer me wrong...but it was lazy. I understand that now and have come to a good place in my personal study...but I'm still lazy when it comes to studying the Word of God.

Now, I must study for myself. The bible tells me to do that in 2 Timothy 2:15. (My prayer is that you would look that up.) I fail miserably at that task.

I am an avid you-tuber and watch a lot of sermons by people much more studied than myself. I'm careful who I watch and always seek the Lord's guidance. I also read (and study) a hard copy bible. Those tasks satisfy the requirement to study but I am still not as diligent as I should be, as I allow other things to take up that time.

I am often amused at the googlers of wisdom, particularly politicians, who use the bible as a source of wisdom...then take every action opposed to its intended lessons.

Then, there are those who defend themselves and their sinful acts, using completely out of context verses and translations that cast more doubt than actual wisdom...

But my job is to turn in the direction of truth...the only truth being Jesus...because He said He is the way, the truth and the life and I believe that because in my 68 years, there has never been a greater truth uttered.

My other job is to pray for our leaders...especially when they announce that they are doing something "prayerfully' because I see nothing from their example...nothing that comes out of their mouths as truthful...and certainly there is absolutely nothing that could be considered wise or particularly judicious.

Discernment is a spiritual undertaking. It requires more spiritual guidance than merely searching out supportive verses and announcing prayerful intent.

But here, I'll let you read that for yourself!

1 John 4:1-6

"Beloved, do not believe every spirit, but test the spirits to see whether they are from God, for many false prophets have gone out into the world. By this you know the Spirit of God: every spirit that confesses that Jesus Christ has come in the flesh is from God, and every spirit that does not confess Jesus is not from God. This is the spirit of the antichrist, which you heard was coming and now is in the world already. Little children, you are from God and have overcome them, for he who is in you is greater than he who is in the world. They are from the world; therefore, they speak from the world, and the world listens to them.

Piece of Cloth

The shrapnel flew so fast
He barely felt it in his thigh
He kept on moving forward
Tears and sweat mixed in his eyes.

He had to stop. The pain too great
The weakness came on fast.
The blood trail quickly turned to pool
The shadow now was cast.

They wrapped a piece of gauze
Around his leg to stop the flow
The blood soaked through too fast
He heard the medics whisper "No!"

He grabbed the nearest arm,
The Chaplain's sleeve, because he knew
That probably he'd sleep here
His days were nearly through.

"Tell my wife I love her, Chaplain!
Tell her what I did!"
Make sure she knows I loved her
And stick close to the kids."

And so it was, they shipped him home
Beneath that piece of cloth
That soon would be his family's
Only measure of his loss

His mother placed her hand
Upon the medals that he wore
That uniform so straight and clean
She loved him to her core.

His wife reached out and laid her hand
Upon his valiant breast.
She kissed his forehead gently
As he laid for final rest.

His dad once more brought out
The tear-soaked handkerchief he kept.
He tried to hide the tears
But in the moment, there; he wept.

His kids both missed their daddy
They didn't yet understand
Why mommy clutched that piece of cloth
So tightly in her hands.

So, when you see that piece of cloth
Still waving o'er the land.
The proper thing to do would be
To touch your heart with hand.

Now we lay our son to sleep
Another brother's grave.
A father and a husband gone
Too soon and oh so brave.

That piece of cloth that binds us all
Beyond the graves of those
Who die wherever they are called
Our freedom is their rose.

And if you have a claim against this
Piece of cloth we share
Then make it now before your God
But if to me, don't dare!

Conquerors.

SOMETIMES IT'S THAT little bit you have left...and sometimes you have to fake it... but you do it because so much depends on it. It's who you are and if you don't face it down, you're not nearly as bold or courageous as you think you are.

The last people you want to let down are those for whom you pray so you just rush into it. You don't let the others drag you down because they're mere mortals. They're not forged from the same steel... They're not a weapon that God wields. They haven't been tested by fire. They're the innocents. You are given to protect them from the beasts that overwhelm them. That's your job...You were born to do it!

So, you get down on your knees and you place your head on the covers... You sprawl your hands out and grip the spread like it's the only thing holding you between this world and the next... because it is...

Your voice shakes. Your hands tremble You anguish because can't go any further with the burden. You cry out "Dear God! I really need your help!... I can't do this alone. You're going to have to build me up. Stir that fire in me, Lord... Give me the courage of my convictions...See me through this!"

That's when the confidence starts to mount and you begin to understand that God has this and you don't...It's not your fight. That's when you see this Goliath from the clouds... You look down from above the fray and you realize that this was never a giant at all... because your God doesn't have any giants.

Your God is bigger than all of it... All of it... It was never your battle to begin with. God brought it to you just to show you that you need him. You have one job and that is to submit to His will rather than bear it all yourself.

You are indomitable when you submit to the will of Almighty God. There are no demons. There are no circumstances out of His control. There are no unsolvable problems. There are no obstacles He can't navigate. There is only one will. His will... being done on earth as it is in heaven.

You ask it all in Jesus' name...the name above every other. You have fought the part of the battle that was yours to fight. You are stronger, confident, courageous! The results are already in...

You are victorious!

> *Romans 8:37-39*
> *No, in all these things we are more than conquerors through him who loved us. For I am convinced that neither death nor life, neither angels nor demons,[b] neither the present nor the future, nor any powers, neither height nor depth, nor anything else in all creation, will be able to separate us from the love of God that is in Christ Jesus our Lord.*

Warrior

THE SMELL OF pitch and oil permeated the air. The flaming arrows had rained down for what seemed like hours. He examined his shield, then used his sword to break off the ones that had penetrated the leather shell.

He loosened the strap on his helmet and worked his head around to release the stress of battle. The adrenaline drained from every pore. His breast plate and belt were suddenly heavy. The garment beneath soaked with the sweat of a conqueror. Still, he stood...

Sheathing his sword, he turned and began to make his way back to the encampment. It seemed a long journey back to the shelter of the tents and the friendly fires. Soon, the smell of roasting meat would replace the stench of battle. The groans of war would turn to shouts of victory.

He had been on his feet for days with little rest. The campaign had lasted months. His feet ached from the tight straps tugging at his calves. He looked forward to the rest. He looked forward to the comradery

He bowed his head and thanked God for once again seeing him through the struggle of men against powers over which they had no control. He was trained for battle but surely his strength had been multiplied. He could see the tents in the distance...Great clouds gathered around him... He began to make out shapes...

That's when he saw the angels...

Ephesians 6:10-18

Finally, my brethren, be strong in the Lord and in the power of His might. Put on the whole armor of God, that you may be able to stand against the wiles of the devil. For we do not wrestle against flesh and blood, but against principalities, against powers, against the rulers of the darkness of this age, against spiritual hosts of wickedness in the heavenly places. Therefore, take up the whole armor of God, that you may be able to withstand in the evil day, and having done all, to stand.

Stand therefore, having girded your waist with truth, having put on the breastplate of righteousness, and having shod your feet with the preparation of the gospel of peace; above all, taking the shield of faith with which you will be able to quench all the fiery darts of the wicked one.

And take the helmet of salvation, and the sword of the Spirit, which is the word of God; praying always with all prayer and supplication in the Spirit, being watchful to this end with all perseverance and supplication for all the saints—

Soldiers Don't.

HARVEY BARRACKS, GERMANY, Dec.30th, the day before the New Year, 1982. I'd been drinking most of the day, off and on...I'd made it through another Christmas by taking other people's duty so they could be with their families. Those who had their families with them deserved that. I'd been in Germany for about 2 1/2 years so I was pretty well acclimated. Not much got to me.

So, this was my holiday celebration, lonely as it was... just me, a few German dunkels and a collection of albums that reminded me of home. It seemed a good way to relax after days of double duty...

I found out I was going to be a dad a few days before. I had no idea what that meant. I thought about it a lot though. I had questions and no one really to ask. So that was weighing pretty heavy on my Infantry brain.

I'm not sure what got me started... I opened the double Dutch windows and sat on the sill facing the parade field, holding the next casualty in my war on Bavarian beer...'Twas the season to be jolly... The second floor wasn't that high, maybe 12 or 15 feet from the ground.

It was cold as usual, with a pretty good dusting of snow, more than most Georgia Boys should ever have to contend with, but that was the work...I sang along with the "Poco" album on the stereo...Last song... Then... silence... deafening... like I hadn't heard in a while. Not something you hear on a military base very often, particularly one with an airfield.

Then, I heard it in the distance, bouncing off the snow like it was specifically meant for me. "Georgia on my mind." the Willie Nelson version. I felt my heart swell. What the...? I imagined home. Suddenly, I missed it... everything about it... My old friends, my family, my dogs... just everything...It was like a stampede of memories...Everything coming at me all at once.

I looked down from my perch and watched the tiny drops fall down and turn into bigger circles in the snow, burning their way to solid ground... Tears... actual tears falling two stories right between my boots as they dangled from the window. It wasn't something I completely understood... I wasn't normally an emotional guy... Maybe it was the beer... Maybe it was the loss...Maybe it was the uncertainty... Maybe it was just too much time away...

I dealt with it like soldiers do. I gave it a minute and then sucked it up... because that is what soldiers do. I got up, wiped my face, closed the windows and put on Statesboro Blues like I should have done in the first

...'cause soldiers don't

Y'all pray for the troops out there. This is a tough time of year for them. Many haven't seen their family or friends for far too long. They go through more than you know.

Soldiers Don't.

No One.

No one knew he'd dragged the mangled body of his buddy down a mountain that had no name, in the middle of a place he couldn't pronounce... knowing full well his friend had died the moment the bullet ripped through his chest.

No one knew about the hardships they'd faced, the stories they'd told the night before or the times they'd laughed and reminisced about home. No one could.

****

No one knew how she wept inside for the young man on the table whose arms were nothing but raw meat and jagged, splintered bone, his face showing only the shock and excruciating pain that comes with sudden dismemberment.

No one knew she'd muffled her own scream as she sewed him shut, shot him full of morphine and wrapped him in enough gauze to get him to a real hospital, somewhere outside this hell they called "the zone."

No one knew she'd be sweating through her bed sheets night after night, haunted for months after her tour, seeing every one of those faces over and over...bolting upright in her bed and shivering until sunrise... No one could.

****

No one knew the terror this thrice deployed soldier experienced when his legs were shattered by the i.e.d. He'd almost expected It. The odds were just too great. He'd had months of practice having seen those before him suffer the same fate. He knew just what to do... Still, the shock of seeing his legs separated from his body caused him to pass in and out of consciousness. He still dreams about it after all these years...The prostheses are still painful but he's learned how to cope they say...'"cause he's tough as nails" they say.

****

No one knew that moment when the snipers bullet tore through the skull of his childhood friend as they shared a smoke in the makeshift tower on the outskirts of some God forsaken village. His own life flashed before his eyes in that moment and for months after he returned home the last time. He's able to function now. The medication is taking its toll though. He just needs to buckle down and keep this job and hope no one trips the wire... the one that holds him together... the one that keeps him from going the way of the others. No one else gets it... No one could.

****

No one knew that they would each take their own life. No one knew because no one cared enough to share a cup of coffee or a conversation... not even a prayer for a guy who was a little odd and struggled to engage those around him... or a young woman who shied away from the crowds... and the faces...or someone with mechanical limbs who struggles still to drink their coffee or tie their shoes.

****

It's Veterans Day. Some folks wear their military patches to announce their service. Some give away poppies or march in small town parades. Some visit graves of their fallen brothers in arms... Some place wreaths... Some salute... Some kneel at the marker and remember.

But some sit at home and try to put on their shoes. Some stare beyond the visible because they still see things others could never imagine. Some are begging for a way out... away from the dreams and the faces and the sounds that haunt them...away from the noise and the voices and the memories...

Find a veteran today and listen to them. They've got stories...and even if they don't want to tell them, they need someone to just be there to stare out the window with them. Just be there...

God bless every single one of my brothers and sisters who dared to put on the uniform, swear the oath and salute the flag of the greatest country on earth!

God bless America and all those who continue to serve. Know that you're someone today and no one can take that away from you... NO ONE!

Stones.

THIS COMPLETE CHARADE that calls itself media...this unelected, self-appointed "fourth estate" who deride the very principles that made us free and expect us to toe whatever line they draw in the desert sand because they alone are the protectors of all that is good.

... this politically biased and totally unaccountable slough of indignant, self-absorbed prostitutes who hinge their character assassinations on their own morally imbalanced view of progress and spread it through their own wealth of interconnected sewers.

... this embarrassingly fixated, flawed machine that supports the defamation of men and the subjugation of women to their own definition of justice and concocted fairness, held together by a web of deceit they refer to as "diversity, " ever mindful of their favorite watchword "equality" as if that were an attainable goal...

... these ever present, glass house residing, purveyors of prudence who demand the attention of millions yet use their sacred right to operate freely, as a weapon to deny others their inherent rights to speak, gather, worship or defend their own interests or pursue their own happiness.

... these seditious instruments of chaos who use their prestigious station to call out the privilege of others by their skin color or social standing who would dare to succeed or attempt to expose their valueless, usurped power.

... this self-appointed conglomerate of mere men who use their vast theater chain to anoint their model celebrities by giving them a forum from which to voice their disdain for the very people who made them famous...

... this corrupted palace of court jesters who empower millionaire athletes to speak the language of foolishness as if to deem their provocation "reasoned" or "fair" or "moral,"... these efforts allowed by virtue of their Sunday afternoon ability to provide a national "hail Mary" according to some preposterous hatred for the flag of our fathers to whom they owe a debt of gratitude, thus relegating those who fought and died to the realm of short sighted, uneducated, "supremacists" who never really understood their "plight." yet somehow provided them a path to economic success.

... these educators, these apologists for failed government systems that historically indoctrinate children and create death and destruction in their path...promising a better world free of greed and other human frailties, in order to create an environment from which a few may dominate the many...constantly stoking the youthful fires of those who abide their folly, giving rise to a burning mass of hatred for the only system of government that has ever allowed free men to remain free.

... these perceived holy and much heralded priests, these predators of free men, these calculating examiners of all things righteous... these inventors of deceit, these discounters of hope, these profiteers of doom...

These are the accusers, the thieves of liberty, the invaders of truth, the scoundrels who regurgitate their singularly produced lies.

They ignore a just God and place their will above His as a measure of their own greatness.

There is little virtue among them... because they are men... men who, when provided stones, will invariably cast them at the sins of their neighbors rather than launch them at the great Goliaths that devour our way of life or build a mighty temple to the one who provides it.

Men who, like all of us, will stand before the one, true living God at the end of the day...and be judged as they have judged... by the only Judge of men.

> *James 5:9*
> *"Do not complain, brethren, against one another, so that you yourselves may not be judged; behold, the Judge is standing right at the door."*

Carpenters.

YESTERDAY, THERE WERE generators and chainsaws... trucks back and forth... people talking over everything...sledge hammers and drills and stacking of wood...carpenters extending our seawall creating a barrier and channeling the water from the lake to a more convenient outlet.

Today, the only sound is a lone woodpecker tapping at the trees in the wetlands... The water is still. The temperature has cooled to the low 70's. It is a glorious day, complimented by the companionship of my wife who shares most of these moments. We are at peace.

The day advances quickly as we make plans beyond the sipping of our coffee and the resting of our souls. We stare out at the water from our chaise lounges on the porch...glancing occasionally at the wood line to perhaps catch a glimpse of the feathered carpenter.

The sun breaks through and causes us to adjust our seats a tad to avoid the glare...We both enjoy the calm...We feel the power of the sermon we just heard; the word of God still fresh in our hearts... We turn our faces toward heaven and worship the One who brings calm to all the commotion...

Tomorrow, different trucks will come loaded with pavers and sod and artisans. They will once again shatter the calm with the hammers and engines that create drives and retaining walls and landscapes.

But today is the Lord's Day...the day we set aside to worship the Carpenter who calms the soul and brings peace to the clamoring noises of men and machines and birds alike, moving us all toward the place that He prepares for us.

Thank you, Lord for calming us in the midst of all the noise... and for the love of the Carpenter who died and rose again... and who now prepares us a place in eternity.

> *John 14:3*
> *"And if I go and prepare a place for you, I will come back and take you to be with me that you also may be where I am."*

The Door

He'd fallen asleep watching the TV again... He woke up a little thirsty and wondered why everything looked so foggy... He looked around for his glasses and couldn't find them anywhere so he decided to make his way into the bedroom without them.

He could barely make out the clock but it appeared to be flashing four zeros... 0000...so he guessed the power had gone out.

He reached for his walker as usual but it wasn't there. He decided to make his way by holding on to the furniture and the door trim. It wasn't that far from his chair to the TV. He'd managed before. He'd be fine.

He stood up and noticed his rickety legs weren't shaking. They always shook... What the heck? He reached for the TV stand, crossed the kitchen and stepped toward the door... Odd... His legs weren't hurting at all. That was a great feeling. He'd been through so much with the neuropathy... but he could suddenly feel them.

He noticed his wife wasn't there. He figured she was out in the sewing room working on something. He didn't call out...She'd be mad if he got up without the walker.

He opened the door to the bedroom and saw them as clear as a bell...They were kind of hovering above the golden floor They just kept saying, "Holy, Holy Holy." They encircled a man sitting on a throne whose familiar voice he immediately recognized.

Without hesitation, the man on the throne said in the most calming voice he'd ever heard, "Stan, we've missed you!"... He knew then. He recognized the voice. He'd heard it all of his life.

That's when he saw his parents. He responded with tears because he realized he was finally home. There were his brothers and sisters and all those friends he missed...The whole scene was lit by the man on the throne. He could only respond with the name "Jesus."

"Well done my good and faithful servant," Jesus said.

Tears welled up in his eyes. Finally, he'd met his King face to face. He began at that very moment to worship Him...forever...

and that is how I imagine my father's passing into heaven...just walking through the door… no pain...just passing from here into the eternal kingdom.

'cause the Bible tells me so…

> *Revelation 21:4-8*
> *'He will wipe every tear from their eyes. There will be no more death' or mourning or crying or pain, for the old order of things has passed away." He who was seated on the throne said, "I am making everything new!" Then he said, "Write this down, for these words are trustworthy and true."*

Power Play

HE EXPLAINED IN great detail that destruction would surely be coming if we didn't act... "It's time for us to take this matter into our own hands," he demanded. "We literally can't take any more of this indecision! Diplomacy has failed!" Slamming his fist on the desk he declared in no uncertain terms," War is imminent!" The time to act is now!" He heard the finality in his own voice..."Well played," he thought to himself.

The red light on the camera switched off. He leaned back in his chair and grinned." Sound serious enough? ...Think I got their attention?"

"The phones are ringing off the hooks," the producer piped in over his earpiece. "Yep!... Looks like we've got ourselves a real war this time! This will be in the news cycle for months!"

He gathered his notes and moved off set. Slicking back his hair, he made his way out of the studio allowing his security detachment to clear a path. His aides began shouting at the paparazzi as soon as he got through the revolving doors. His personal assistant began briefing him on the world leader's responses as they headed toward his car. They were all outwardly furious, naturally. Actors in a play. It profited them to play the game but he knew they were on board. He'd directed the entire event.

The inquiring shouts pulsed through the crowd. "Senator! ... Senator!... Can you tell us anything more about the war...Senator Powers?"...He stooped to enter the car as the microphones jabbed at the windows like cattle prods. He held up his hand as if to say,

"No further comment" He busied himself with the internal conversation as they sped away.

The frenzy had begun. He had no time for any of them today. It was time to get this party started. Let them chew on it awhile and make all their foolish predictions. He'd have an all-out war by evening. He'd show these imbeciles what kind of power he wielded. He was through talking!

None of them knew that the weapons had already been armed and were within minutes of striking. Sure, there would be a short-lived resistance...but he would smash that quickly. All the proper channels were opened. His allies were stacked and properly compensated. The favors had been extended. The time was right. This had been planned from the very beginning...Now came the final blow. It was now...or...

> *Revelation 16:16*
> *And he gathered them together into a place called*
> *in the Hebrew tongue Armageddon*

Ground Control

WE ARE ALL control freaks in one way or another...We actually think we control our own destiny...We're careful to eat what is good for us, exercise when we can and practice healthy habits (by and large)...Our doctors keep us on a regimen of vitamins and medications that help us maintain healthy attitudes so that we can...live longer...

We insure ourselves and our families against every possible event...as if to shield ourselves from any fate that might befall us...because it is the "responsible" thing to do...We're uncomfortable with handing over the reins to anyone else...We can't imagine dying because we have no control over that...and we know it...We try to ignore the inevitability of that..

Those who have witnessed a lot of death "experiences" often talk about the different "styles" of passing away...Some folks just take a bold step...courageous and strong...Some, tired from the battle just go to sleep...Some fight to the very end and go out guns a blazin'...

But all succumb...give up control...End...

We don't talk about it...and dwelling on it isn't really something we enjoy...but considering it, even if it is uncomfortable, is a necessary burden... otherwise we are ill prepared for that moment when we are forced to give up control...that instant when we hand over the reins...We must ask ourselves to what and to whom do we succumb? and who can we trust in that moment...

There is only one who gave his life for us and rose again. I know of no other who professes to have had that experience. I know of no other who can breathe life. I cannot imagine handing over the reins to anyone else when I come to the end of my life here on earth...because the promise is that I will continue to dwell in a place He has built for me...

I'll hand over the reins to the one who comes back riding a horse... Who better?

For your consideration...

> *Jesus said to her, "I am the resurrection and the life. The one who believes in me will live, even though they die; and whoever lives by believing in me will never die..."*
> *John 11:25,26*

Name and Number

You kneel with faux conviction
Showing absolute disdain
For those who came before you
And for those who still remain.

Your boorish exhibition
Resurrects a solemn past
While somewhere in the world today
That flag flies at half-mast.

You cannot know or understand
The spirit of that flag
Unless you've held in both your hands
A young one's worn dog tags.

Or watched a mother clutch it
When they hand her what remains
Of her forever soldier
Who shares her family's name.

Or watched their tearful children's
Eyes still swollen from the crying,
Gazing at the coffin draped
Not understanding dying.

We've seen our sons and daughters fall
Beneath those stars and stripes.
They've gone now to their Maker
Having sacrificed their lives.

They watch your cold irreverence
Their legacy prevails.
They took that flag to freedom
The stories they could tell...

Of freezing cold and sweltering heat
They each remember days
When strength had left their bodies
That banner still, they raised.

The bombs burst all around them.
There was no crowd to cheer.
They inched that banner forward
Through bullets, blood and tears.

You dare to denigrate the flag
That commemorates these fallen
To list your petty grievances
Before you go footballin'

So, know that when you kneel there
Your honor takes the hit.
Real heroes up in heaven
Aren't likely to submit.

These purple hearted warriors
Fully valiant to their end
Care not for your dissension
Nor the message that you send.

Your different colored jerseys
Don't mean much to them at all.
They've taken more than you can dish
By answering the call.

So, kneel away and take your stand
Announce your grievance loud.
Just not to those who paved your way
They're watching from the clouds.

And in your silent moment
With the cameras aimed just right.
Think not that you are warriors.
You're not even in the fight.

Your feigned commitment to the cause
Of righteous indignation
Carries not a single ounce
Of weight to their citations

And know what God has knit together
Can't be torn asunder
So, when you kneel remember this:
He sees your name and number

Wing and a Prayer

THE SHORT STORY of the "forgotten" falling man of 9/11

He stared out the window as he did every morning since he'd started working at Marsh & McLennan...sipping his coffee and perusing the day's financial spreadsheets, the never ending, unrelenting spreadsheets.

He loved it up here on the 95th floor. He could see almost the entire city from his left of center office...She was massive, teeming with life...daring to be New York City...arrogantly preparing to crank out a new day without a hint of fear. Lady Liberty down there doing her welcoming thing...sturdy, confident... The ships steaming in and out of the harbor...Start spreadin' the news!

The view never got boring... Only the financial reports could do that ...All that changed were the numbers. His job was to identify any anomalies. The numbers went on forever. He considered them job security and he knew them all too well. It was tedious work but it kept the kids in a good school and the wife in decent dinner wine, so he faced the challenge daily. It was a good life all in all.

Just as he turned away from his screen to head for the copier, he saw the plane out of the corner of his eye. It looked like it was coming in awfully low but he'd gotten used to the constantly stacked planes circling the airport ...They sometimes played tricks on the...wait! ...

"Nah!... Couldn't happen in a million years" he said under his breath... Still, It came... growing larger and larger...and faster... He froze...Everyone did! It was more than surreal... He didn't want to be the first to point and yell...What could he possibly say that would make any difference? It happened in a flash.

Then... slow motion... The nose of the plane plowed into the building, slicing through like a javelin heaved from a great distance. The earth-shattering explosion instantly sucked the air out of anything and everything ...He watched the wing take out the windows and saw the engine as it plowed through everything in its path. The metal twisted so quickly it was impossible to recount exactly what had happened. It all just became a mass of twisted steel and concrete dust...In a millisecond most everything disintegrated...vaporized.

The screams came from everywhere but he could barely hear them over the roar of the jet engines still whining and pulsating around him. The concrete dust and shattered glass were blinding. There was no real center of gravity...no absolute, no stable point from which to operate...There was only chaos... complete, utter chaos... Literally nothing was where it stood 10 seconds ago.

The screams grew louder, piercing the space now twisted and battered beyond recognition...There was a strange odor that overwhelmed all the rest. Clearer minds would have deduced that it was jet fuel... but for now it was just a part of a total sensory breakdown... Nothing... absolutely nothing made sense. It was just a fog... like some crazy dream sequence out of a movie. He walked toward the loudest and closest scream just a few steps away. There was a lady there, writhing, unable to move beyond uncontrolled gyrations

It was Sheila Adams, Mr. Thomas's Administrative Assistant. She had the corner office and shared the biggest view of the city. He recognized her face, sort of... but not the grimace. She was twisting violently as if something was churning inside her body. He grabbed her hands in an effort to stop the motion, whatever it was. That's when he saw the beam. It had bent nearly all the way across her body and had pinned her in place... Both her legs were dangling in space...space outside the shattered glass...No matter the effort, he could see that her end was imminent.

She had no control over her legs. Clearly, her body had been crushed by the beam. Her legs were convulsing as a result. The look on her face was somewhere between disoriented and horrified. She reached out as if to say, "Just keep holding onto me." So, he did just that. He didn't know what else to do. Pulling her up was impossible. She let out what would be her final agonizing groan. "Jesus!" he heard her say...Then she appeared calm. She passed quickly.

He stood for a moment trying to digest what he'd just witnessed, having experienced the dying gaze of a once pleasant woman he'd passed in the hallway every day for months. He was in shock. He strained to see through the debris...something, anything that looked even remotely stable.

Shaken but still aware, he thought of his kids and his wife. He wondered how long she'd wait dinner...He smiled at the thought. He took a moment to remember each of their faces. He understood that he may never see them again. He wondered how they would tell them. That thought crushed his spirit.

That's when he felt the heat... like a blast furnace on his back. He heard more screams but they died down quickly... The heat was unbearable. The flames started to lap at everything around him. His skin started to blister from the heat. He knew he couldn't bear it for very long. He saw the others losing the battle. He stood in a literal oven, realizing his fate. The only way up was down.

As a final release of the last bit of his human energy, he moaned aloud... "Dear God! What is this? ... Forgive me, Jesus!"... and he stepped out of the window... because there was nowhere else to go...There was no shielding from the heat...At least he'd have time to pray...Of all the endings he'd imagined, this was never on the list. Who could imagine such a horrible thing?

He plummeted toward the ground at remarkable speed, praying to God for grace and mercy for his wife and children... and asking for forgiveness in the short time he had left. He just wanted it to be over. He opened his arms as if to fly.

Suddenly, he was floating... not falling at all...The wind felt good on his back... Dust and debris washed over him like a soft sea spray...He saw the gates...He felt the warm glow of a soft and reassuring light. He was immersed in something that could only be described as... love... Not just any love... but THE love... the Love of God.

In that instant, he was eye to eye with the man he knew to be Jesus. He'd met Him a few times...as many had. He remembered the day he'd invited Him into his life. He hadn't been as close as he should have been...He knew that now. He recognized the peace. He also knew he was home.

And there was Sheila... plain as day...not a scratch...smiling and welcoming him with a friendly hug... He'd watched her horrible death just moments ago. She thanked him for his compassion. He told her that he wished he could have done more. That's when Jesus smiled as if to say, "Nothing you could have done would have taken her out of my hands." This was Jesus... King of Kings... Lord of Lord's...and this was eternity... forever...and there was no doubt, this was heaven. It wasn't the end... It was the promised beginning.

The End... of the beginning of forever

I pray that your journey offers you the peace only Jesus can provide and that you too, will ultimately land in the arms of a loving and generous God who sent His only Son to pay the price for your transgressions. There's no greater love than that!

> *Corinthians 4:17 & 18*
> *"For our light and momentary troubles are achieving for us an eternal glory that far outweighs them all. So, we fix our eyes not on what is seen, but on what is unseen, since what is seen is temporary, but what is unseen is eternal."*

Meanwhile...

THE BURGERS WERE perfectly shaped and marinated. Every condiment imaginable lined the serving table. His tools and squeeze bottles were conveniently located. The time was right. He threw the meat on the grill and popped open his first beer of the day. All the prep work was done. The grill and the neighborly conversation would take care of the rest.

Meanwhile...

He was adjusting his chin strap when everything exploded. Pieces of the vehicle ripped through the interior. Shards of searing metal flew in every direction. Instant chaos...The entire driver's side of the vehicle all but disintegrated, including its driver, Pfc. Rich "Richey" Hardeman. They'd buried the i.e.d. in the dune, face high for maximum effect. Maximum effect was achieved.

Meanwhile...

His neighbor Charlie came in through the back gate with a giant bowl of his now famous 'tater salad. As usual, he greeted him with a slap on the back and the always expected yank on the apron string, causing him to retie it yet again. Setting the covered salad in the middle of the picnic table, he sniffed the smoke from the burgers, feigned hunger and greeted Cheryl with a friendly half hug. It was all part of the drill...the annual Bay Street Memorial Day celebration

Meanwhile...

The metal ripped through his flak jacket like it wasn't there. The Humvee was tossed like a toy and threw him against the door with a force that could only be described as gut wrenching. The sound was crushing, deafening. The concussion sucked the air out of everything in an Instant. The certainty of it was all too clear.

Meanwhile...

More neighbors gathered. They talked about the last fishing trip and shouted at the kids not to dive into the shallow end of the pool. The smoke billowed from the grill. The sun danced... The pool shimmered...The conversation became a dull but light hearted roar. It was a beautiful repeat performance, a perfect sequel to last year's festivities.

Meanwhile...

The pain wasn't immediate... He saw the damage to his arm and felt the deep laceration in his neck, right at the carotid artery. He knew from the deep red color of the blood that he wasn't going to last long. The red blotches quickly covered his maps and pant legs. He knew it would be over quickly. He thought about his kids, too young to be without a dad. He shivered a bit. He was cold...in the desert...not a good sign. He was bleeding out.

Meanwhile...

The burgers began to sizzle...The aroma brought everyone closer to the table. Laughter rang out mixed with reminders about minding manners and warnings of consequences for the kids who didn't follow instructions. It was a great day on Bay Street.

Meanwhile...

Sergeant Thomas Pritchard took his last breath in a place no one had ever heard of, for a cause few understood anymore. He wouldn't be remembered except by a handful of friends and family. His last action was to grip the flag on his sleeve and form his wife's name on his parched lips.

Meanwhile…

When it was time, Cheryl cut the watermelon into sections and distributed it onto the paper plates already stained with hamburger grease and tater salad. The red blotches quickly covered the newspaper laid down to absorb the mess.

The phone at the Pritchard house rang but no one heard it over the celebration. The message machine picked it up. They knew Tom wouldn't call for hours. He'd be busy briefing his team. It was night in that horrible place. He'd call after his patrol. The annual Bay St. Memorial Day celebration would continue...

Meanwhile...

Patricia Hardeman sprang bolt upright in the bed. Richard thought she must be having another nightmare, but this time, the look on her face was different. She couldn't hold back her scream. "Richeeeey" She knew! Dear God...She knew!

Happy Memorial Day, indeed.

> *John 15:13*
> *Greater love hath no man than this, that a man lay*
> *down his life for his friends*

The Appointment

WHAT IF TODAY wasn't about you? What if it was about someone else? What if an appointment had been arranged for you to meet someone and your only job was to tell them how to get to heaven?

What if the entire day came down to one chance meeting...one conversation...one smile...one nod...one opportunity?

What if....Just what if... Almighty God had purposed for you to have a conversation with someone who is lonely?...or deeply saddened?...or angry?...or hurting... or just too distraught to continue?...What if that person was someone you loved?...or a family member?...or a close friend? What if you were the only thing that stood between them and heaven? What if it was their last day on earth?

Could you talk to them about Jesus? Could you show them the way to heaven? Could you take advantage of the opportunity God has provided? Could you tell the story?

Could this Jesus actually be the way, the truth and the life? Could all of this stuff you've heard about Jesus paying the price for your sins be real? Could it be that all you have to do is accept that He is who He says He is and ask Him to forgive you for your transgressions? Then, what if He actually writes your name in the book that insures an eternal future in heaven?

Each day I pray for an opportunity to tell someone the good news that we can all get to heaven from where we stand...Each day God arranges for me to speak to someone about Him...We refer to these meetings as Divine appointments...It amazes me how God provides us with those opportunities. Maybe you don't believe in them...

Or maybe you've just had one...

> *Mark 16:15*
> *"Go ye into all the world and preach the gospel to every creature."*

Postcard—Day 4 of Mini-Vacation. Pandemonium!

APPARENTLY, THERE IS a law against turkey tacklin'... WHO KNEW?...There was about 10 that came into the wetlands so me and Lynn snuck up on 'em to see how many we could grab...I was one up on her when the Game Warden showed up and started yelling like a bull moose in a thunderstorm...So we let 'em go and waited for him to settle down...A fat man like that shouldn't get so upset...and let's just say it was humid and he was plum shiny from sweatin'

Anyway, we got him settled down enough to write us a ticket... but then I asked him about "evidence" and he went off the deep end again...I wasn't looking forward to resuscitatin' him because of that mouth to mouth thing ...so I just shuddup and leaned on the car...Lynn went and got him some tea so he sat on the tailgate with us for a while and talked...He decided we was good folks and tore up the ticket...We shook hands and he got in his cruiser and was headin' up the road...

Just then, I saw Lynn pull back on that slingshot rubber and sail a rock a good 30 yards an' hit oneo'dem turkeys dead in the wattle... took his head off clean...right in front of the Game Warden's car... Lynn let out a hoot and I bout busted a gut...We took off runnin' like a coupla' jewl'ry store robbers

You could actually see the car twerkin' like Miley on meth...I saw Ol' Warden Babbleduck clutchin' his chest and trying to spin that car around like that bald-headed feller in Fast and Furious...

We doubled around and made it home safe about sundown...I swear that girl ain't right...We hafta keep the lights off in case they come lookin' for us...We ain't stopped laughin' since...We're still havin' a ball here...S'all good!

Free advice

It's not what you know…It's who you choose as your teacher…

Learn about mercy from the healed…

Learn about gratitude from the wounded.

Learn about trust from the abandoned.

Learn about peace from the warrior.

Learn about love from the heartbroken…

Learn about wealth from one who has lost everything…

Learn about thrift from the generous.

Learn about courage from the meek.

Learn about prayer from a survivor…

Learn about wisdom from God.

> *James 3:17*
> *"But the wisdom that comes from heaven is first of all pure; then peace-loving, considerate, submissive, full of mercy and good fruit, impartial and sincere"*

The Color of Privilege

I WOKE UP IN America today... There's a lot of opportunity for a person like me... I can do whatever I want, really. I can work wherever I want and make money however I choose, as long as it's not illegal...Opportunity is all around me...

I can sing, and write and worship God. I can love and laugh and be with my family. I can learn to play an instrument. I can learn to dance or learn another language... but most importantly, I can learn!

I can sleep at night. There are people out there who are keeping me safe... men and women dedicated to the cause of serving their communities by protecting me... literally serving and protecting... Me!

There's also dedicated men and women stationed all over the world serving as my protectors...standing in the gap between me and whoever seeks to harm me. I appreciate what they do. I can't understand people who don't.

I can build things...anything really. I can build roads and bridges and houses and skyscrapers. I can build machines that do anything but mostly I can build a life... There are obstacles of course, but I can overcome them. They're just obstacles.

I can excel... I can decide what my upper limits are going to be and strive to be the best. It doesn't matter what I choose because this is America...Land of the free...

I am so fortunate...So privileged!

I am most assuredly graced by God himself

What color am I?

Confiskated

I REMEMBER MAKING A skateboard out of one of my sister's roller skates and a piece of 2x4 ...It was an awesome project with lots of hammering and other man stuff.

I also remember riding the skateboard into the sewer at the bottom of Clifton road at about Mach 5...I definitely remember dark blue shins, a badly lacerated knee that needed a few stitches and elbow scrapes that bled for weeks.

I cannot help but remember explaining to my sister that I had used her skate. She was really mad that I wouldn't go back down into the sewer and recover her roller skate. There were a lot of bugs and snakes and rats down in there. Sheesh! A man can only do so much.

Months later I built up the nerve to retrieve the skateboard. I distinctly remember pulling up the manhole cover with my friend Ricky and observing the now heavily stained piece of wood. Attached were some very rusty metal roller skate wheels. I remember climbing down into the sewer and grabbing the slick stained piece of wood from out of the goo and acting as if it were nothing at all. Truth be told, it was terrifying. The skateboard, if you could still call it that, was in pretty bad shape...but somehow, I was relieved to actually have it in my hand.

I remember talking to my dad about how best to make it look better so I could surprise my sister with it. I remember offering to give up my allowance for whatever we would need to bring it back to its original luster. I remember my dad telling me that it was too damaged to restore...something about the ball bearings. Technical man stuff but still disappointing.

Soon after, I remember my dad taking me to Archie's Army store in East Atlanta where we purchased another pair of skates, my sister's size. I remember how good it felt to be doing something that she would appreciate and how good it would feel to finally make amends for my selfishness.

The look on her face when I gave her the box was worth every bit of the trouble. I sheepishly told her I was sorry that I took her roller skate and used it for my own purposes. I told her I wouldn't do that again. She was good with it. We weren't exactly friends at that age, so it was an event for one if us to do something nice for the other. She was happy with her new skates. These had boots attached so she wouldn't have to rent them at the Misty Waters skating rink. That was kind of a big deal back then.

I still received my allowance that week. (Indeed, a lesson in grace) Mostly, I remember my dad actually sitting with me on the back steps and using the entire event to explain to me about repentance and how we all need to do that now and again...not just because it makes us feel better but because God wants us to do it.

He explained how we need to forgive each other and how important it was to ask God for forgiveness because when we sin, it's against him...He went on to tell me how repentance cleans us up and makes us more presentable. It reconciles us to a right relationship with God. He told me how God wipes the slate clean. He removes our sin from us "as far as the east is from the west." I remember thinking, "How perfect is that?"

Confiskated | 125

When we repent, God immediately forgives us. That's what Jesus did for us. He took our sin on Himself and made it possible for us to reconcile with God. Because He is God. It is through Jesus' work on the cross that we have the ability to reconcile with God.

There's not a better feeling than that this side of heaven. Knowing that Jesus loves us and wants to forgive us is central to knowing him. He has given us a way out. He promises that he will forgive us if we confess our sin and turn away from it. That's how it works. That is the reason for Jesus' sacrifice.

> *1 John 1:9*
> *"If we confess our sins, he is faithful and just to forgive us our sins and to cleanse us from all unrighteousness."*

New England

GETTING CATAPULTED BACK to Florida today... This was a great visit! We've absorbed a wealth of history...and a grandbaby fix that probably won't last the winter...These are some busy folks up here. I'm thinking we'll be back to camp here in the Spring if all goes well. Would love to see the reenactment of Lexington/Concord on Patriots Day.

Personally, I love New England. There is history and charm at virtually every turn. I'd like to walk through a few of these battlefields but time won't allow. History bleeds here. It captures the imagination and begs your personal involvement. This is where it began. This was the lab in which the American experiment was concocted. Americans need to see and understand what happened here. It's a "must see."

The beaches are beautiful...They're everything you'd imagine from the lighthouses to the rocky shorelines. The fishing villages are "as seen on TV. " It is all very picturesque and appeals to my own sense of discovery. It's a great place to wander.

There was lobstah, chowdah and octopus...I did not partake of anything with tentacles as it tends to squirm about on the plate. Those who did seemed to enjoy it. I assured them all that they were welcome to my portion. It seemed fitting. I gave them the same look they give me when I offer them possum stew... It's a two-way street.

The people here have been welcoming. My "New York" accent caused more than a few inquisitive looks...particularly at restaurants. Sometimes I'd ask, "Do y'all have grits?" just to watch the expressions. All in all, though, we were well received. Lynn speaks fluent Yankee so I was in good company.

No witches were burned during our stay... No cannons were fired and no tea was tossed. There was however, reveille every morning from the local Air Force Base and Taps at night. Can't say that I didn't welcome that. It was a time of reflection, for sure.

And... I can now actually say that I went to Harvard and received little or no education...

So back to the lake and the sunrises. It'll be good to get home and reflect on our visit. I'm sure I'll write a bit more detailed report... Perhaps it's time to start the Christmas letter...

Heart...To Heart

EACH YEAR, THE obligatory annual checkup (or some new aggravating condition) drives me into the doctor's office for the lab work that will decide my course of treatment over the next year...the results of these tests deciding which medications will be added to my daily regimen of life saving miracles and keep me above ground, as if that were the main objective.

Being of relatively sound mind and aging body, I answer the questions as they are posed, being wary of which ones will cause my health insurance premiums to rise and which ones will open the door to those gendarmes who seek to mark my mental condition as decidedly doddering and take away my license to drive or shoot or run with scissors...

I give up my four vials of blood and half cup of urine to my now favorite nurse Gail, who never misses the vein and handles the sample cup as if it were a silver chalice, placing it into the "to go" container with great care. I watch her label all of it ensuring that there are no visible possibilities of confusing my offering with that of the vagrants and horse thieves who frequent the same multi-physician offices...but that's just me being me.

I don't sweat the small stuff because I realize that God has the whole of my chemistry in His very capable hands. I am not given to worry or fear or hypochondria, so I await the results with limited trepidation. It's a few days wait but I busy myself and the time passes quickly.

I don't know what it was that called my attention to it but when reading the five pages of my lab reports, and listening to my doctor's insightful oral report, I was suddenly overwhelmed by the delicate balance that has been maintained for these 67 odd years and how little adjustment has been required. The words "fearfully and wonderfully made" were whispered into my sub conscience. My heart swelled with gratitude.

As I drove the few miles home, I sang the 1st verse of "How Great Thou Art," the same verse I had sung the week prior when driving to submit my fluids for examination. This was a moment of praise and worship that I would have missed, had I not been grateful for a good report.

That's when I felt somewhat embarrassed, convicted really, by my own self-indulgence. I was drawn to a place of prayer for those I knew, who rarely get such good results...and for those who were suffering due to a chronic medical condition or who might not really grasp the wonder of it all or the magnitude of God's grace and mercy.

I was immediately aware of the intricate demands of my own body, the delicate measure of my now ethereal thoughts and the immeasurable power required to manage all of creation...Somewhere in that deep rumination, I submitted to what could only be termed as an invitation...a call so clear and immediate that to not answer would be considered defiance.

I pulled my truck into an empty lot overlooking the lake not far from my home and stared toward the place where the sky glances off the treetops. I knew where I was. I'd been there before. I watched the clouds curl up into the sky, their floating being yet another source of wonder. I approached the Throne...because I was called there. It was time for my eternal checkup

Then, I was granted a moment at the altar...that place of tearful gratitude... that humbling observance that comes from the presence of Almighty God...that place beyond the horizon where the mighty fortress stands...that strong tower...that unshakable, immutable forever place where a righteous and holy God searches the hearts of His children...that brush with eternity that causes us to close our eyes to the world and reckon with the Creator of it.

I prayed aloud, head bowed on the steering wheel, now listening to my own heartbeat that had suddenly become louder as if it were purposed, beating in response to an everlasting drum, ignoring the earthly measure of its rhythm and the life-giving pumping of my blood. I presented myself to perfection recognizing my own complete lack of it. I was without excuse, a sinner submitting to the will of his Father...a lone, repentant man seeking favor from a holy God.

I was forgiven for my transgressions...all of them...because the one in whom I had placed my trust years ago, was able to remove them from me. My checkup was complete, the results issued by the author and perfecter of my faith.

There is a place where every hymn you've ever sung and every bible verse you've ever read meets the reason for their existence. It is the place where Love extends His nail scarred hand and walks us into the place called Glory...where the only light is His and the burdens of your heart are rolled away...I trust you will answer the call to meet Him there. I pray without ceasing that you will.

Thank you, Almighty God, for those you send to care for us and for your ever-present word...and for the songs you place in our hearts. You alone are worthy!

> *Proverbs 17:22*
> *A cheerful heart is good medicine, but a crushed spirit dries up the bones.*

To Russia with Love

DEAR MAMA,

Zdravstuj!

I feel I have made a grave mistake in coming to this America. Our news agencies there in Siberia don't even come close to explaining this culture. I cannot begin to explain this confusing, complicated people. Many of them are rich but they are extremely unkind, unlike my fellow Siberians.

They wake up every morning and go to their favorite restaurant, McDonalds...They get their Mcbreakfast and move in great numbers from one line to the next. They stand in line for everything yet there is no shortage of food nor is rationing necessary. There is an abundance of everything...Still they wait!

They take their children to schools where they are forced to wait in lines throughout the day. The children are targeted by mass murderers in what is known as "Gun free zones." Clearly their education system has failed but they have yet to realize that the main reason for the attacks can be blamed on the fact that the shooters of their children can't read. They cannot read the No Gun Zone signs. I have decided that most Americans are illiterate. They claim to have many rights but don't understand them. They're allowed guns but don't use them.

Their men are somewhat effeminate. They put their hair in buns and flit about with their phones and backpacks as if on their way to the market. They call themselves "millennials" as if there is sanity attached to that moniker. They smell remarkably like the French except that they bathe regularly and scent themselves. I detect a hint of watermelon and vanilla in their presence.

I should not have chosen to attend culinary school. Hunting is forbidden here and the markets are all indoors. Food is shipped in via trucks and frozen for the most part. The women shop for food while the men read their lists and stand in the aisles trying to make sense of all the coffees. There are a lot of angry chefs, one Mr. Gordon Ramsey being their leader. He is a creative man but sadly insane. I do not aspire to his level of success. He is a terrible example of service.

They abhor violence yet their streets erupt whenever they have political differences. Drugs are rampant yet guns are blamed for the violence. There is no rhyme or reason to their infighting but always their media is heard in the background, inciting them to race wars and gender wars and political faction wars. That seems to be the function of their media, to start internal wars.

The women gather en masse to condescend the men. They complain of glass ceilings and unequal pay yet you never see them like in Siberia cleaning the bear meat or making the borscht. They wear hats that would warm their ears in winter. Instead they color them pink and wear them to simulate their private parts. They are not embarrassed by this display.

Unlike in Russian sports, their men compete against their women provided they have opted for certain surgeries. They always win. It is very confusing. They all receive trophies but the neutered men are always the winners. It's like they think the energy comes from their man parts rather than the training of their muscles.

On Sunday they take their children to church where they are taught about God and receive sex education. This too is very confusing. I have not been able go discern how the two intersect. Suffice to say it is an odd relationship amongst the religious.

They claim to be the richest country in the world yet their people live in tents in their largest cities. Their war veterans are homeless and must beg for food. They throw out large amounts of cooked food from their restaurants yet there is still hunger. There is a company called Waste Management but clearly no one understands that concept.

They believe Russia interfered with their election yet they allow migrants to vote in their elections without identification. This is devoid of any reason or logic. I don't think they understand their own system of government. Many of them love our Vladimir Putin more than their own benign President Trump. They neither understand greatness nor tyranny. They are a sad people.

Their Congress are genuinely disinterested in the people. Many of them, somehow elected by the people, speak out against anything that would cause America to move forward. These are called progressives. There is no accounting for their definitions.

A portion of the people hate their President because he is a successful American businessman and he represents the people well. Others wear red hats to identify with him but groups of news cameras and gangs gather to remove the hats. I have not seen evidence of this "freedom of speech" we've heard so much about at home. Clearly their love of country has disappeared due to their great division.

It is good to be Russian. At least we know the State will survive us even if we die drunk in the snow. Americans have no such hope. When this generation passes, it is impossible to predict their survival.

I want to come home! The vodka here is too expensive and the women have two eyebrows...and small bones.

I am sure there is a better place for me there in Siberia. I will not miss this America in the slightest. It is dangerous and dirty unlike our Russian paradise.

Tell Svetlana I have learned to make the Chic•fil•a she enjoyed when she visited here. The workers there were the nicest people I have encountered during my stay. I find it difficult to carve the fries properly but they taste the same. I look forward to creating this and serving it at our family get togethers.

There is so much more to talk about but I must go now. I only have a few more episodes of Iron Chef to watch before returning to the Iron Curtain...ha ha!

Искренне

IskrenneYour сынок, Boris

I Love To Tell the Story

IT'S NOT AN easy conversation.

It's just not... Trying to explain the love of God in a world full of people that deny His very existence requires that you do a lot of backtracking...If every part of the message is contested, it's difficult to navigate your way back to love...

If you try to explain the existence of God to an unbeliever, they'll invariably throw so many wrenches into the conversation that you have to spend a lot of time drawing parallels and responding to the "Why would God" questions... Then you move past all the comments about the "Eye in the sky" and "man upstairs" thing and of course there's the "Science ultimately answers every question" which it never does, ordeal. It becomes an arduous journey, a painstaking, detailed presentation. Christians are often ridiculed and their message seldom welcomed. Many give up. They make excuses about their own inhibitions and lack of insight. It's as if they really don't feel obligated to share the message because of the backlash.

People have genuinely hardened their hearts. We have to accept that...If you face that kind of adversity with a flickering, unfocused light, you won't last long in the court of acceptance. Your job is to constantly appeal and impress and advocate on the side of your Father. That is why it's not called simply the commission... It's called the Great Commission. It came from Jesus' very lips so yes... It's for you!

> Matthew 28:18-20
> And Jesus came and spake unto them, saying, All power is given unto me in heaven and in earth. Go ye therefore, and teach all nations, baptizing them in the name of the Father, and of the Son, and of the Holy Ghost Teaching them to observe all things whatsoever I have commanded you: and, lo, I am with you always, even unto the end of the world. Amen.

Still, the job is to navigate all of that without flinching and without hesitation. It is an important message with eternal consequences. We can't imagine that at the time we're telling it but God stirs the heart. It's important to remember that...We can't save anyone. All we can do is present the age-old story and try to piece together a pattern that interferes with their preconceived notion.

I talk to people about Jesus. I use whatever tool is available to me. There are 66 books available and a plethora of Christian books that help us make our story exciting.

My story isn't dull... because Jesus isn't dull...Heaven won't be dull...

If I could share a couple of things that have helped me in the adventure of telling others about Jesus, I think it may help others to share the message...

When I came back to the church after many years of befriending bartenders and perfecting my drinking, pool and dart games, it came to me very quickly that I had forgotten many of the Bible stories I'd heard as a child. One day it occurred to me to go into the church nursery and peruse the children's books they had there. No one could see me so I was free to take my own refresher course. That experience not only caused me to reestablish my basic Bible knowledge but it allowed me to simplify my message to others. Children's books don't require a degree in divinity. They are stories that cultivate interest...as well as your faith and a relationship with Jesus.

Later, when I began to study the Bible more deeply, I read this...

> *Matthew 18:2-5*
> *"And He called a child to Himself and set him before them, and said, "Truly I say to you, unless you are converted and become like children, you will not enter the kingdom of heaven. "Whoever then humbles himself as this child, he is the greatest in the kingdom of heaven."*

Another great influence for me, aside from regular Bible study, was a constant review of the Baptist Hymn book. Just reading the words put me in a place of worship... of praising God and listening to His still small voice... I still do it from time to time as the songs are still available online...but there was something about those old hymns that stirred my soul. Some I remembered right off... Some caused me to remember my musical training so I could read the music and find the melody.

That's where I learned to hum hymns...Sometimes I still hum them to the Lord. Sometimes, I start to tear up when I think of all the folks I've seen singing those songs... my dad... my grandmother on piano... church friends who've gone on to be with the Lord... not because I'm sad, but because I know I will join them in the Lord's time.

Then I read this:

> *Colossians 3:16*
> *Let the message of Christ dwell among you richly as you teach and admonish one another with all wisdom through psalms, hymns, and songs from the Spirit, singing to God with gratitude in your hearts.*

The Appearance

WHETHER YOU BELIEVE in Him or not, God is who He says He is. Living your life according to His plan is sometimes a difficult thing to do... not because God isn't consistent, rather because we are not. Still, trusting God is part of that process. Sometimes, we're reticent to trust Him because we fall into that guilt and unworthiness thing or we're unsure of what God's plan actually is so we tell ourselves we're trusting God but we haven't really let our plan go.

If all that makes any sense, then here is a bit of a story that was so affirming and so perfectly timed that I was literally stunned by the miraculous presence of God. I sat in a room with Him. I was somewhere between completely humbled and completely awed. I knew that He knew... Everything.

It seemed a small matter. Still, the Lord knew it was important in my life and used that instant to affirm not only that He heard me... but that He was actively working in my life.

A bit of background is in order. Living at the lake is truly a wonderful experience. Nature is a constant source of entertainment and of course there's a wealth of wildlife here in Northeast Florida. The view is breathtaking often accented by storms moving in off the coast, along with brilliant, morning sunrises. It is, for my wife and I, a perfect place to retire.

In close proximity are quite a few house trailers clustered together around fish camps and small businesses built to cater to the lake population. Most of the trailers were initially getaway places for folks who enjoyed lake life. Later, they became rentals and of course many were ultimately used as a source of income for people getting on in age. Years of long-distance care and do it yourself maintenance caused some of the trailers to become a bit more dilapidated than many of the newer home owners deemed acceptable. They were thorns in the sides of property values.

Such was the case with the one directly across the street from us. It was an eyesore and the original owner had moved away. The people who bought it had no concept of what is required to rent a property and simply lowered the rent to accommodate whoever wanted to live there for whatever time they had the money to rent. It was a place for transients used solely for a source of income for the owner...Out of sight, out of mind.

You can imagine the types of people we encountered there. It was the perfect drug house, isolated with perfect vision up and down the road...along with a perfect view of my newly constructed retirement home. I spent nights monitoring the all hour's traffic and plotting my move if any dangerous activity got out of hand. I'm from Atlanta... Fear wasn't my motivation... protecting my family and property was... I was duty bound in that regard.

I had spoken with the local Sheriff and the owner of the property... the former unable to do very much and the latter not necessarily concerned. It appeared as though we were indeed, on our own. We realized that this was a considerable problem and that we would need to address it head on when the timing was right.

I began to pray. I prayed that we wouldn't have to be on constant guard and that God would provide a way for us to come and go without having to be concerned for our belongings or our safety.

We gave control over to the only one who could intervene on our behalf. It became our prayer for the years before we moved into our chosen place of retirement. In the interim, the mobile home next door to the nuisance house came up for sale. It was atrocious. We were able to buy it at a nearly salvage-level price. We rebuilt the on-site garage, demolished the trailer and built a cottage we now use as a guesthouse.

We moved into our home in December of this year. We settled in and monitored the house across the street as was our custom. A young couple moved in with their baby. We were a bit relieved and a bit concerned as we knew a bit about the condition of the home. Still, we prayed.

One day recently, as I went to the mailbox, the lady who owned the house approached me and told me she wanted to sell the property. I was of course interested but then she told me the price she wanted. It was completely beyond our budget and way out of line with the comparable prices in the area. She was nice enough to allow us to get an inspection and an appraisal. We then made an offer that was less than half of her quoted price. We doubted there would be any interest in our offer. We continued to pray.

The next day, I woke up with all of this on my heart and mind. I made a special plea to the Lord for wisdom. Then, I sat down with my Bible and read the first chapter of Proverbs in order to refresh my knowledge of what is and isn't wisdom. I sought the Lord's will and became familiar with the words "Thy will be done." which is always the end of any proper negotiation.

On the coffee table was a bookmark given to us by one of the ministries we support. I unwrapped it and put it on the page I had just read. I resigned myself to accepting the Lord's answer, whatever that was. I closed the Bible preparing to mediate on the passages I had just read. I was indeed staring at the cover when suddenly, within a millisecond, my phone lit up and vibrated on the table. It was a response from the property owner who explained that she thought the offer was too low but that she was prepared to accept it. There was no lapse in time and no second guessing. It was perfect timing by a perfect God who isn't bound by time...but is the Creator of it.

I welled up with tears sensing the Lord's presence...My heart was about to beat out of my chest. I pointed skyward and announced my praise and thanked Him for His timely answer to my prayer. I didn't much care that I had gotten the deal I wanted. What I cared about was that I had caught a glimpse of Almighty God...that He had indeed been with me all along, through every prayer and every decision about the property. I realized then that He was there with me in my living room...not that He wasn't always but there was a special presence...an immediate and wholly awe inspiring, definitive presence...so close as to cause me to tremble. I don't tremble often. I could only raise my hand and point to heaven. I cannot, and will never be able to describe that encounter. Human words are insufficient. Suffice to say that I was made aware in a very real way that God was in fact, guiding this entire matter... Reassuring, comforting, certainly affirming...

The entire event has unfolded in a way only God could administrate. We signed the contract yesterday. I know that for whatever reason, I am in the center of His will. Any doubt that I may have had is completely and irrevocably steadied in that thought.

I'm not here to explain God's intentions... I'm just here to announce that I am grateful for the blessings He so generously bestows. I can't possibly explain the nature of this answered prayer. I can only acknowledge that it was absolute and individually wrapped... It was offered by an all-powerful, very real, very present God...so much so that it could not be mistaken for coincidence or happenstance. It was a uniquely personalized gift from an ever present, infinitely creative God...as if the moment I actually accepted His conditions, I got an immediate "Yes."

I'm not sure of exactly what we'll do with the property but for now, there's a whole lot of work to do and a young couple there that needs a little direction and a lot of help to go forward in their lives. We've decided to be examples to them. Lynn is making them a spaghetti dinner as I write this. We will begin our journey tonight. God sends you people... Sometimes He sends you, people!

There's more to this story. There are lives involved and personal relationships to develop. There's still a lot of work to be done. There are many other matters yet to be negotiated... but I know this and no one can shake this foundation. My God is ever present, worthy of praise, righteous, holy and loves me beyond anything I've ever known or ever will. That is the only truth I can offer beyond His capacity to save each of us from an eternity separated from Him.

> *Psalm 145:3*
> *Great is the LORD, and greatly to be praised, and his greatness is unsearchable.*

Endlessness

ETERNITY IS THE place that should be encouraging to us but it is often the place where we draw the line between reality and imagination.

For me there is no line of demarcation. I believe in the one and only God who is eternal, unbound by time, everlasting...I believe in forever. I believe in a life that goes beyond what I see because I have an inherent desire, indeed a longing to meet my Creator.

In the literal sense, forever can't exist for some. They know only of a world they can see and feel and touch. Anything beyond that is fantasy...the stuff of science fiction.

Yet the God of the bible resides there. In fact, He is everywhere, all at once and has always existed in a realm beyond even our ability to determine exactly what that means. We cannot possibly understand an infinite Creator using our created, finite minds. We can only observe the inestimable measure of His vast ability to create.

He created tangible beauty in this world for us to see feel and touch, indeed an ever developing, repopulating, robust natural environment that points to His own omnipotent ability to provide a perfect environment for His wondrous creation.

I also believe that He created in each of us a yearning to see beyond ourselves, indeed a desire to see Him...to experience Him...to analyze and discover not just His existence, but His propensity to create beauty and life beyond our own imaginations.

I believe we all have a desire to peer into the unknown. That is why we look beyond the oceans, past the horizon, into the vastness of space, beyond even the stars and into the uncharted distance.

In our efforts to see further and further, we build giant telescopes and great vehicles to transport them, all to gaze into the darkness, the heavens, as it were. We feel a need to know what is beyond our touch. We want to go there. It would appear we are indeed drawn to heaven.

Could it be though, that we are drawn to the one who lives there, this God, this omniscient being, this great designer, this Creator of all that is observable? Could He have implanted in us, the desire to know Him?

I believe that the appetite to discover is an innate part of our makeup, our search to establish that life exists beyond this few decade's span... an affirmation that something or someone awaits us.

I believe that an intrinsic and necessary, natural hope demands that we seek to extend this life beyond this ever-declining physical body.

I believe in the soul. I believe in its perpetual existence. I believe it needs fuel for the journey beyond this life.

I believe that the bible is the living word of God. I believe it is the only source by which we can actually view eternity. I believe that Jesus came so that we would have the hope that lies in Him. I believe He is, as He says, the way, the truth and the life...and that no one comes to the Father except through Him.

I believe that an infinite, loving God who causes us to seek eternity, would also present us a vehicle and a map on how to get there. I believe that the bible is that map and that Jesus is the means by which we can travel to a timeless eternity.

> *John 14:2-4*
> *"My Father's house has many rooms; if that were not so, would I have told you that I am going there to prepare a place for you? And if I go and prepare a place for you, I will come back and take you to be with me that you also may be where I am. You know the way to the place where I am going."*
>
> *1Timothy 1:17*
> *"Now to the King eternal, immortal, invisible, the only God, be honor and glory for ever and ever. Amen"*

Good Stock

My grandparents were immigrants...They came over from Tallapoosa, Georgia. . . what you might term "country folk" ...They picked up and moved all the way to Atlanta...They had to learn "big city" ways...They had to learn because it was how they would survive...They worked...hard!. They bought a home on the outskirts of town. My grandfather was a railroad man and a preacher... They assimilated and raised 10 children on their own...without government assistance...because there wasn't much, if any...

They never mistreated anyone...They were kind to their Indian neighbors (The Najars) and bore no animosity toward anyone. If they did, it was never spoken...People kept their opinions to themselves in those days...

They went to church. He (George) to teach and preach...She (Nancy Pearl) to play the piano...They were Christian people. Never overwhelmed by the drama of the day...Nose to the grindstone...Trust God...Love thy neighbor...Help the needy...All of that...

Their children (my uncles aunts and dad) were raised "in the nurture and admonition of the Lord"...They were taught how to pray and read the bible. They understood that we all depended on God... and that he was good.

George (who only had one eye) and Nancy Pearl sent 5 of their sons to war so that they wouldn't have to learn German or Japanese... The sons were encouraged to do their duty...They all came home from the war...All of them...as did some of their future wives.

My grandparents believed in God and the reality of answered prayer. These sons, war heroes all...married and raised their children to be self-sufficient...It's just who they were...

We did as our parents before us. We strayed from home and rebelled a bit. After all, it was the seventies... but we all came back into the fold as we came of age...some sooner than others...

I am one such second generation immigrant... I can never remember being poor...I can remember being hungry a couple of times... lonely at other times...or too tired to go very much further on occasion...Life was a battle...but something or someone, always made me trudge ahead...There were times I needed to just dust off my boots and deal with it...So I did.

We each made our way...We asked for nothing except the good graces of God Almighty. We knew from whom all blessings flowed. We never thought of government as anything but a place to pay taxes.

Many of my cousins served in the military. Some are liberal minded...some conservative...Some Republicans...Some Democrats...Methodists, Presbyterian, an Eastern religion or two...We are mechanics, teachers and artists...We are a pretty diverse bunch...

We are products of a family who believed in God...and his provision...We are independent to a fault...We were fortunate to have strong willed, self-reliant, patriotic, loving grandparents...and parents...The only privilege I had was knowing them...learning from them...and being born in the America they helped build.

I am ashamed that the "American way" is quickly becoming one of dependence on government...rather than dependence on God

Another advantage was being raised in church and being "trained up in the way that I should go."...There is no accounting for good parenting. Right and wrong are still choices. We still believe there are consequences to those choices. God is still in charge.

But privileged?...I can't imagine that I...or anyone in my family had a benefit we didn't earn...What we did have was something the schools don't teach anymore...Resolve...or "Stick-to-itiveness" as my father called it...I can't imagine not having a job or not looking for one. To me, those are the only options as long as I am able to work.

Any privilege I may have is determined by my own efforts and the grace of Almighty God without whom my next breath cannot be drawn.

> *Psalm 121*
> *A song of ascents.*
> *1 I lift up my eyes to the mountains—*
> *where does my help come from?*
> *2 My help comes from the Lord,*
> *the Maker of heaven and earth.*
> *3 He will not let your foot slip—*
> *he who watches over you will not slumber;*
> *4 indeed, he who watches over Israel*
> *will neither slumber nor sleep.*
> *5 The Lord watches over you—*
> *the Lord is your shade at your right hand;*
> *6 the sun will not harm you by day,*

nor the moon by night.
7 The Lord will keep you from all harm—
he will watch over your life;
8 the Lord will watch over your coming and going
both now and forevermore.

Chronicles of Nanner

I COULD SMELL IT in the air as I pulled into the drive
I was dog tired and weak from the struggle to survive
But when I opened the door, I was suddenly revived...

Nanner puddin'

I walked straight to the stove after passing through the den
There my honey stood with a spoon in her hand
Kinda' smirkin' at the sight of my big ol' grin...

Nanner puddin'

There it sat on the counter top, warm
A painting of love from an oath long sworn
Framed in ovenware perfectly adorned...

Nanner' puddin'

It had meringue whipped higher than a milk jug top
Little brown caps like fresh dew drops
All swirled around like circles in the crops...

Nanner puddin'

She said "There's chicken" so I grabbed myself a thigh
Dipped it in some gravy and a biscuit on the side
Told her it was good but she knew that I'd lie...

For Nanner puddin'

I finished up quick as she knew I would
Grabbed myself a bowl and by the sink I stood
For a big ol' helping of all that's good

Nanner puddin'

She dipped that spoon down deep in the muck
Angels started singin' with a chord they'd struck
On the heavenly lyres, from the clouds they plucked...

Nanner Puddin'

Niller Wafer edges kinda' crispy brown
Just a little bit crunchy with crumbs all around
Big chunks of nanner so easily found.

Nanner puddin'

Puddin' so thick I had to wash it down
With a quart of milk and a slurping sound
That echoed through the hall and came back around

Nanner puddin'

Draggin' my spoon on the bottom of the bowl
Lips still smackin' from the depth of my soul
I shoot a quick glance at the cook 'cause she knows

Nanner puddin'

So, I get up slow and head over to the stove
I gaze at the love in that great big bowl

and there it sits just a little bitty hole in

Nanner' pudding

Damage Control is nowhere near
I'm focused like a laser on that yellowed veneer
Nothing between us but air and fear

Nanner' puddin'

I scoop up some more and head over to my place
My wife looks over and says "You forgot to say grace"
And I know she sees shame from the look on my face

Nanner puddin'

So, I put my spoon down and I ask the Lord
To forgive my gluttonous, self-centered hoard
And thank Him for all that He helps me afford

Nanner puddin'

Then slowly I doze into puddin' hibernation
Calm and peaceful, kinda' sweet sedation
Weary from the rigors of a great celebration

Nanner puddin'

Now I'm not sure how I'm gonna' die
But I know this, when in the coffin, I lie
There ought to be a spoon 'cause I know that On High

There's Nanner puddin'

And I know that at the end of those Heavenly feasts
There'll be a moment of complete and perfect peace
When all are calmed including the beasts with

Nanner pudding

Why else would God make a nanner tree?
And put together two like my wife and me
To enjoy such a wondrous delicacy…

Like nanner' puddin'

Stuff I Learned on COPS Tonight

EVERYBODY IS A tough guy till the taser prongs go in... Then they make little girl sounds.

Make sure your toothless sister isn't sleeping in the front seat of your car before you go to the liquor store.

Jumping a chain link fence with your pants around your knees defies the laws of physics...All of them!

A conversation between a drunk guy and a cop is a monologue...

Never carry over 2500 dollars in the hood unless you have the keys to the evidence room.

After 2 am... hookers speak in 5-dollar increments...and they're all going to their friend's house...The friend's name is Terrence...

Concrete removes tattoos!

There is only one response to the words "Put your hands behind your back!"

The bleeding drunk guy always loses...

Las Vegas and New Orleans share the same clientele.

Cops can smell marijuana before they get out of their car.

Neck tattoos cause robberies.

If you are driving a car that isn't registered to you, you are a car thief until proven innocent.

The space between your face and a cop's face is entirely his space. Shuddup!

Always wear your teeth when you call the cops…You don't want to be those people on camera.

There are 14 places to hide in a trailer. The cops know all of them.

Cops come in bunches like bananas.

All the pot in the car belongs to the driver. The beer belongs to the passenger…The real drugs are in the girl's pocketbook.

A hooker has a one in four chance of being a cop…an eight in ten chance of having a disease…and a 100% chance of having a drug habit.

It is impossible to plead your case with a German Shepard attached to your leg.

A glass pipe bears no resemblance to a Christmas ornament no matter how many times you say it!

Drinking and driving can only be determined by walking.

Handcuffs impair speech.

A fair fight is one in which the Police drive away with a bloody person in their car.

Drunk people follow their inner stupid!

Kicking a window inside a cop car is not a viable exit strategy.

Don't ever hide in the freakin' shed!

Exposed underwear is a prime indicator of guilt...Dirt and leaves in hair are additional charges.

If you're uncle moves into your trailer, he's selling drugs and blaming you.

Dogs cannot pronounce names...no matter how hard they try.

Brother Cletus Intercedes at Prayer Meetin'

"Dear Lord, I know you know everything about everything and surely I'm not suggestin' that you can't do as you please, but we got some perty serious stuff goin' on here and we can hardly see past the fog of it all.

I would never pray that you should smite our enemies, 'cause we know you could if you wanted to...but we got people down here killin' babies like there's no tomorrow, but for them babies there ain't no today...

We got folks dressin' our children up and confusin' 'em about their body parts and a lot of things they're not even old enough to talk about. They don't even know which bathroom to use, Lord. It's that bad.

There're folks here who think it's okay to have intimate relations with kids who ain't got no direction to begin with. They buy 'em and sell "em and pass 'em around like biscuits at breakfast ...It breaks our hearts to watch it all, Lord.

We need your help, Lord. We need for you to protect our kids. They're bein' born without daddies who care about 'em and mama's who have to raise 'em on their own. They cain't give 'em direction cause they caint be there all the time.

Drugs are takin 'em now cause' they're so easy to get. How does a kid get through all that, Lord? There's less and less of 'em here at church so all they know is what their phones teach 'em...

There ain't no heroes anymore 'cause all these kids see are people runnin around stompin' on flags and cussin' whenever your name is mentioned. They don't hear nobody pray and anybody that tries to set an example gets caught up in a buncha' fanger pointin'.

So, I ain't asking for a smitin' necessarily Lord, but I see where you cracked open the earth a few days ago out in the desert and I was wonderin' if you could just swaller up a few of these heathens just to draw some attention. It may take more than that 'cause we all know there's a lot of stupid out there that we cain't fix, but we need to ask you to protect our chil'ren...'cause the devil's coming after 'em guns a blazin.' We're asking 'cause we know you're God and we ain't! We're all outta' answers.

You know we love you and look forward to the day when you take us all home but for now, we need to put these kids in your mighty hands Lord, 'cause you're all we got left! We've made a mess of it!

In Jesus' name...

Amen"

> *James 5:16*
> *"The effectual fervent prayer of a righteous man avails much."*

At Least

AT LEAST HE could lean against the rocks and watch for any more of them trying to surround his buddies up on the hill. The sun was brutal, as usual...but at least he could still move his fingers. The bullet had gone through cleanly just below his shoulder. He knew better than to move too much but at least he was able to pull his knees up and rest his weapon on them. At least he wouldn't have to bear the weight.

At least he was able to think it all through. He had time. He was sure most of the hostiles were beyond him. He understood that no one would be coming to get him. There was no way for them to know he'd been hit. He could see his own short blood trail, not enough to cause alarm, the wind already covering it with sand... the damnable, perpetual sand. He knew he'd bleed out there. At least there was some shade from the branch above his head.

He was young but they all were. At least he'd loved. He knew she would miss him. She'd hugged him so hard at this last deployment that he almost broke down. At least she'd have his memory and his son...His son...He was really going to miss him. He was growing up so fast and curious about every little... He coughed a bit and struggled to breathe.

At least someone would mourn his death. His mom would take it the hardest but at least his dad would console her, even while his gut churned and his tears bled into his pillow when no one could see. He'd get them all through it. He always did.

At least his wife would remember... and he was sure she would teach the boy. Maybe at a get together they'd all reminisce...somewhere between the hot dogs and the beer someone will remember that time they took the ride up to...He could feel his breath getting shorter...probably the lung collapsing...

Maybe on occasion they'd see the folded flag on the mantle and remember him. At least the boy would have that...and the stories... and the medals. He hoped at the very least they'd celebrate his life and not drag it out. The boy needed to be able to sort it all out.

He reached up with his good hand and touched the flag patch on his shoulder. He knew it was closing in. He was willing. It was worth it. He remembered the Bible verse "greater love... something, something... die for his friends" Why couldn't he remember all of that?

He remembered giving his life to Jesus. He knew he'd meet Him soon. At least he had that ahead of him. At least he'd finally be able to thank Him for His sacrifice...At least he would be able to see everyone again someday in heaven because of Jesus. He hummed a little "I can only imagine." and realized it was far too exhausting...

This is what he signed up for... This is what they meant by the ultimate sacrifice. He'd seen others go...some peacefully... some violently... He wasn't sorry for his own situation. He just wanted to get it done and sad that he had to leave everyone behind. He was already missing them.

That's when the lights went out...At least it was quick.

He died there on that hill, filled with memories so vivid he could hardly distinguish them from reality...At least he thought he did... but there she stood...holding his hand...in what appeared to be a hospital room...

and that's why we can say "Happy Memorial Day" ... because some didn't die... but all would've!

> *John 15:13*
> *"Greater love has no one than this: to lay down one's life for one's friends."*

Shaken Not Stirred

WATCHING EVIL UNFOLD isn't new. There's a lot of it. It doesn't require any particular insight to see that the world is imploding. We predict "the end is near" but we've got to make enough money to be comfortable in retirement so it's..."yeah... That's bad...Gotta' run..."

We watch the news as if there were an end to the story. We check our computers and our phones for updates as often as we can to make sure there is no further "breaking news" that might interrupt our busy day... made busier by the notifications and barrage of instant information that consumes us.

We insert our OMG's and our LOL's wherever we see an opening and corporately shake our heads at all the horror. "How could they?" (insert gruesome video and dramatic music)

We are shaken at the thought that the horror might somehow contaminate our pristine corner of the world...so we have an alarm system and a gun. We've done our due diligence. "Ain't nobody got time for no death and destruction 'round here."

Rarely though, are we stirred to the point of confrontation. We hope there's a God who handles all of this and we "pray" that no harm will come to us personally because we have to have the kid at soccer practice at 3:15 and if he's late one more time, he'll get benched...so "gimme' a break" is the sum total of our prayer time...

At times I have to ask myself, "What if this soul, this being, is so preoccupied that it can't process anymore turmoil? What if we deliberately look past the God of the ages because we believe that we just can't be delivered from the gloom or the doom? What if we've accepted this decay as "the way it is?" What if there is no fix, no escape? There's just fear and madness and corruption...and evil. Everything happens because it's supposed to and nothing we do will prevent it...so ours is to take a deep breath and press on... because the alternative is...well... inaccessible...

What does it take to drive us to our knees? How much energy must we expend crying out to politicians and these so-called leaders of our (ugh) communities? How much blame can we place? How much evil must we absorb before we appeal to the one who created us...before we understand that the only opposition to all the evil is a greater force of good...and the only thing good is God?

Is there nothing that will stir us to the point of repentance? ... Is that word, that action, something we will even consider in our busy, everyday lives? Do we even know what it means to ask God for His forgiveness and turn away from our transgressions against Him?

Is this just a well-intended verse from an antiquated book of wisdom...or is it the only acceptable answer to the evil that surrounds us?

> *2 Chronicles 7:14*
> *"If my people, which are called by my name, shall humble themselves, and pray, and seek my face, and turn from their wicked ways; then will I hear from heaven, and will forgive their sin, and will heal their land."*

Internal Organ

YOU PASS IT every day on your way to work and sometimes on the way to the restaurant in the evening...You tell yourself you'll visit there soon...You reckon there are some fine folks in there who do good things for others. Your friend's mom has gone there for years.

You admire the stained-glass windows...the way the lights shine through them when people are inside. You have no idea what the pictures mean. You'd really like to see them from the inside...probably some bible stories or something.

Once... you heard them singing. You thought for a moment that you and the family should stop in sometime...maybe listen to that young Pastor. You met him once at Denny's...Seemed like a nice enough fellow...Nice family.

You had a friend who visited there... She told you all they did was ask for money...She passed away and left all her money to her drug addicted son. Too bad about his accidental overdose...He was a good kid for the most part...

At the red light you look up at the steeple. You see the cross atop it and wonder how in the world they keep it clean...There must be some fine men there that do such things. But even so, it is beginning to show signs of wear. If you weren't so busy, you would be willing to help with the lawn or help paint...or something.

You've noticed the landscaping has started to fade. It's not as green as it used to be...needs fertilizer...and the flowering plants have long faded...The building could use some paint in some places... The sign is in need of repair...You could help them with that as well...if you weren't so busy.

You remember the sound of the organ from your youth...You wonder if they still have one. You remember that time when your church sang that song..."Old Rugged Cross" you think it was...You remember how it stirred you inside. You remember your mom's tears as she sang it without the hymn book. You remember your own tears when she passed. You want to see her again. She's in heaven though...

The light changes and you drive past...The parking lot is empty except for a couple of cars...must be the Pastor...or maybe the janitor or secretary... Seeing that steeple in the rear view mirror, and that cross atop it, reminds you that it's been a while since you prayed...

You know you really ought to visit. If you just weren't so dang busy. You know the kids could use some direction...They are getting a bit rowdy. You barely remember all the bible stories from Sunday School...Maybe you should...

The cellphone rings...It's your wife...She's been in an accident on the way to drop the kids off at school...The kids are okay but they think your son has a broken arm...The car is smashed up pretty bad and she has some stitches in her brow...but she's fine. They're all fine...You can hear your little girl sobbing in the background... You really need to thank the doctors...

You hang up the phone and make the turn toward the hospital... You still hear the sound of that organ...and you remember some of the words now...

"On a hill far away, stood an old rugged cross..."...yeah...That was it...It was about Jesus...I remember now," you say aloud... We really ought to visit that church...Maybe next Sunday...I just hope they don't ask for money...We're gonna' need a new car...

You think maybe you should pray... but you wouldn't know what to say... Maybe if God spoke to you, you'd know how to approach Him...

> *Romans 8:7*
> *"For the mind that is set on the flesh is hostile to God, for it does not submit to God's law; indeed, it cannot."*

Jot and Tittle

I'M FINALLY FINISHING up that bible everyone's gonna' want to read. I figured why not, since everybody reads the parts they want to anyway.

I took out all the bad parts. especially the misogynistic parts about Eve coming from Adam's rib. It seemed so wrong for God not to create her as an independent woman. So, I changed that along with all that stuff about them both sinning against God. Then, there's the whole talking serpent thing and them realizing they were naked...just not believable. So, I removed that whole story too because that seems to be what started the whole messy, judgement stuff.

Reading about the flood and the plagues and the Sodom and Gomorrah debacle was just too farfetched and seemed a bit homophobic. It all made God appear to be way too judgmental and imperfect, so I fixed that with a new rainbow story. I think you'll enjoy the new pet friendly version without all the destruction. The animals talk and help Noah with the Ark. It's much more family friendly now.

Then, I noticed there wasn't anything about evolution or any proven science so I just made Genesis the Book of Darwin and included some climate change information. I renamed that the Book of Gore, so its all settled science now.

I removed all that stuff about plagues and parting seas and Israelites wandering around in the desert for no reason...not very easy reading and kind of depressing. It's pretty cheerful now 'cause we all know "God is good...all the time."

I changed the Ten Commandments to incorporate a new moral code. It's much easier to follow and includes a Twelve Step program for those who can't stay on the straight and narrow. It's so much more motivating.

As it happened, I had to remove most of the Old Testament because of all those crazy "prophet" dudes and their weird predictions. There wasn't much that was current or sensible, so that made it much easier...

I also had to remove all the references to Jesus in the New Testament except the parts about Him loving us. That was kind of hard because a lot of times He would do stuff like throw people out of the Temple or talk down to his disciples.

I removed the crucifixion part too because it was really gory and horrible, and all those Gospel writers talked about it like it really happened. No one wants to read how God became a man and suffered so much, especially since He took on our sins and became a sacrifice for each of us or that He died on a cross, for goodness sakes... So, I took out all that sinning stuff and made Jesus look more tolerant...and that resurrection thing was just too much so I put in some stuff about diet and exercise because that'll help people live longer.

I removed every single reference to hell because no one believes in that stuff anymore... A lake of fire as punishment? Surely not the God I know. He loves us too much to punish us for all eternity!

I kept some Satan stuff because there are times when we all have to blame someone for our mistakes, and he's a pretty good place to dump all of that. Besides, we all know he isn't real. He's a perfect antihero though, so I decided to keep him in the book.

I also replaced a lot of God's names with Buddha and Allah and even Zeus so no one will be offended. It's so much more inclusive.

All of that revising and editing thinned the book out enough so it's a pretty quick read and makes a really good e-book. I have friends that got through it in about twenty minutes. They all felt better after reading it so it must be good.

I think you all will like it. It's much easier to read and I'm sure God will approve of it now that its all updated. I'd ask Him to write the forward or something but I have no idea how to get in touch with Him. If any of y'all have His email, I'd appreciate a text...and thanks!

Anyway, y'all buy my book. It's called "The Holistic Bible" by Christian B. Ware. If you buy one now, I'll include my newest CD..."Jesus Loves Cats"

And don't forget... I'm praying for y'all...

...and whatever you do... Don't read this verse.

> *"For truly I tell you, until heaven and earth disappear, not the smallest letter, not the least stroke of a pen, will by any means disappear from the Law until everything is accomplished."*
> -Matthew 5:18

Buzzards

WE EXPECT THAT our enemies will transgress against us and they invariably do. Sometimes there are so many enemies, we put up our defensive shields and determine that they all are equally offensive and must be defeated. It's our nature not to let them win...at anything... ever...It's a war of wills. They must be crushed! They are enemies who have crossed a line in the sand. We never really forgive their betrayal. We leave the bones so we can pick at them later... like buzzards.

Our friends, though... the ones we love deeper than we ever tell them...the ones we trust to be with us when we go up against the giants...the ones that have sworn allegiance by virtue of their longevity or their infrequent offenses...the ones in our inner circle who hold our deepest secrets, must not be allowed to slip into the category of enemy." When they fail us, even if it is an innocent oversight, we tend to demand a little more from them...a deeper apology, a longer period of reconciliation, a reminder of that time when we assisted them beyond reasonable expectation... because that's who we are...likewise, so should they be...That's the unspoken rule of loved ones. Tit for tat, quid pro quo. Yet even with these, we reserve the right to pick at the bones if the need arises...like the buzzards.

Like it or not, we place limits on our forgiveness and apply it on a sliding scale as if we alone are capable of dispensing the proper portions according to the severity of the offense. We'll save the memory and use it to multiply the charge for the next offense...In effect, we leave a bone to pick...like the buzzards.

In reality though, that's not forgiveness at all. That's just dressing the wound. It only stops the bleeding but the wound is still open... the bones still exposed and unburied. We'll return to them if need be and pick them clean...like the buzzards.

Thankfully, that's not how Jesus forgives us. We are forgiven so completely that it is as if the offenses against Him never occurred...Our transgressions are "washed as white as snow." We are all offenders...every single one of us...guilty of the sin yet graciously forgiven.

That is an awesome thing to think about and a great example for us all...to allow ourselves to forgive one another beyond the scope of any offense...to forgive as if nothing ever happened... to love at a level created in heaven beyond our own human capacity...to forgive our friends and enemies at the same level...to leave no bones to pick...separating ourselves from the buzzards...

Indeed, It is a blessing to the offender and the offended, to enjoy peace without the burden of returning to the offense...to accept that we are all guilty of transgressions against a holy God and to recognize that we too require complete, perpetual forgiveness... to remove even the bones and reinstitute the conditions we are commanded to observe by Jesus himself, to "love thy neighbors as thyself." Without forgiveness, we can't possibly achieve that.

Charles Spurgeon explained it like this...

"To be forgiven is such sweetness that honey is tasteless in comparison with it. But yet there is one thing sweeter still, and that is to forgive. As it is more blessed to give than to receive, so to forgive rises a stage higher in experience than to be forgiven" and of course, the timeless wisdom of this...

> *"If you forgive others the wrongs, they have done to you, your Father in heaven will also forgive you. But if you do not forgive others, then your Father will not forgive the wrongs you have done."*
> *- Matthew 6:14-15*

As if...

THEY ARE LAUGHABLE, these discussions of moral equivalence.

...these ongoing comparisons to moral behavior as decided by presumably powerful people

...these invented arguments that cause division for the purposes of staining reputations so that power can be ripped away from one camp and given to the other, based on some national acceptance of right and wrong.

...as if these very comparisons to historically evil figures are the gauge of what is and isn't moral.

...as if national leaders are our guide to what is and isn't good or evil by virtue of their election by a righteous people...

...as if one administration prevails over another because they each follow some preordained moral star that sets them on a higher path to righteousness...

...as if the judges of morality are the writers and celebrities who have somehow attained a higher plot of moral ground by virtue of their fame.

...as if we sit on the precipice of goodness, teetering on the edge so that all it will take to curse us all with a permanent place in hell, is an executive order or a misdirected action.

...as if we each dare not align ourselves with a righteousness developed in a foul-smelling cauldron by those "other" power seeking deviants.

...as if truth itself is decided by our political choices and lies are determined by our opposition to them.

...as if no good can come from a leader who is determined by his opposition to be immoral.

...as if evil is determined by some group think or that goodness is measured by our uncorrupted vantage point.

...as if our morality is created by those who draw the lines from their own stinking, back room closets.

...as if we can be led to moral high ground by attaching ourselves to any agent born in darkness and raised in the light of a quest for wealth and power.

...as if the forces of evil would only invade the one faction and leave the other to generate only goodness...

...as if there isn't a real Judge who is the perfect arbiter of good and evil.

...as if this were never written:

> *Romans 2:1*
> *"You, therefore, have no excuse, you who pass judgment on someone else, for at whatever point you judge another, you are condemning yourself, because you who pass judgment do the same things."*

Stuff My Dad Actually Said.

"I THOUGHT I told you to shut up at least 3 years ago!"

"Don't you be here when I get back and don't you be gone!"

"You're adopted… like a puppy…Your mama let you in while I was at work. If you had wandered up to the house when I was home, you'd be in the woods somewhere eatin' barely dead meat."

"The difference between me and you is about 2 feet…When that gets down to a few inches…There WILL be a test."

"Your mama don't love you like I do…You should thank God for that every single day."

"Don't hit your sister in the stomach…because…never mind…Don't hit your sister."

"Oh yes…You CAN talk back to me…but I'll be walking down the church aisle… gripping one of the handles on your box!"

"You're going to see the Beatles because your sister is going to see the Beatles! if we don't take her, we won't be able to live here anymore!"

"Because she is your mama!… Sometimes I don't like her either!"

"Boy…Don't make the police come here and draw a chalk line around you!"

"We buy your clothes at Sears. We will always buy your clothes at Sears. When you outgrow Sears, you can buy them yourself!"

"Shuddup when you're talking to me!"

"This ain't Perry Mason…I can't run and hire a detective every time you lose your jacket. Keep up with it!"

"Because God made you my son. If you were someone else's son in Zimbabwe, you might not have to go to church… but we go to church!"

"Why do I even buy you books? I should buy you a huntin' knife and a loin cloth and just let you loose in the woods!"

"Your socks do not have to match your shirt! Wear longer pants and no one will notice!"

"Haircut or throat cut…Your choice!"

"Pretty soon you're going to figure out that it ain't all about your happy. It's about your mama's and your sister's happy. Your job is to get out there, get married and make a mama…then make her happy!'

The Earth is Round. Weather is Cyclic and God Ain't Dead...

It seems odd that we have to re-teach the simple things but as I talk to people, I realize that they aren't really attached to any concept of absolute truth anymore...except for one inescapable truth...No one gets out of this life alive. That's enough to start a conversation.

The depth of any inquiry regarding that fact becomes provocation for some level of response. No one wants to appear blind to the possibilities of an eternity so the thought engages them at a level that requires a thoughtful response.

There is no universally accepted answer to "Where will you go when you die? The response to that inquiry is always interesting because it dares to question the one thing that no one wants to talk about... their own mortality.

Saying" Jesus" in a public place outside the walls of a church is tantamount to yelling "Fire" in a crowded theater. It provokes many and calms few, depending on the audience. It is "the name above every other name" and therefore requires an acceptance or a rejection of an eternal relationship with Him. The consequences of that name being an eternity spent in a literal heaven or a literal hell.

Still, the answer to the question of eternity lies solely in Him. He will be the Judge in the end. You will face Him, bow before Him and confess that He is Lord. That is an eternal and absolute truth. How you settle that in your mind and heart is a matter of your own pursuit of what is and isn't truth and your decision based entirely on the question Jesus Himself asked..."But what about you?" he asked. "Who do you say I am?" (Matthew 16:15) The answer having eternal consequence.

How can I be so sure?... because I have answered that question. I have searched for the answer and settled the matter. There is no wiggle room in my decision. I no longer wonder about my own outcome. I have an inexplicable peace about my own future. My effort now is to extend that effort beyond myself and invite you to settle the matter. I have accepted that my eternity will be spent in heaven because of what Jesus did on the cross and not by my own goodness. I have accepted not just a truth but what I believe to be the truth. I have accepted Jesus as the one who holds that future in His mighty, capable, loving hands.

> *Philippians 2: 9*
> *"Therefore God exalted him to the highest place and gave him the name that is above every name, that at the name of Jesus every knee should bow, in heaven and on earth and under the earth, and every tongue acknowledge that Jesus Christ is Lord, to the glory of God the Father"*

The Atheist's Kerfuffle

Your transgressions are yours to keep. You wear them because you must. They are a burden because there's no place to put them, no one to forgive them...They are yours to suffer. Some days you wish there really was something bigger than yourself just so you could share some of the load. You tire of the heavy lifting...

You can't cry out when life overwhelms you. It too, is a burden. The kids need shoes, the car is failing and the medicine isn't working like it once did...You can't keep up the pace. You're working harder every day but the money doesn't stretch far enough...You need a break but there's no relief in sight.

Wealth abounds yet it is just out of your reach. You are thankless. How could God?... You erase the thought. You watch as the world passes. No one can hear your whimper. You cannot complain because that would strengthen the case against your pronouncement that there is no touchable, hearable, seeable God!

You can't love completely because you only experience life at an emotional level. You think you know what it is but you can't possibly...because God is love...but you reject that as well. You work hard at love.

You fix everything yourself because you believe that's a sign of strength...except that things remain broken. The world as you know it, is fixable under its own power... You imagine yourself a builder, a visionary, a self-starting vehicle for change and a doer of great things. Now, all you have to do is convince the others... but they don't listen.

You have no everlasting...no view of eternity...no shelter...no fortress... no shield...It's you... Just you...Alone with your thoughts... because you have demanded it. How dare this God require you to submit to His wishes...

You dismiss those who try to bring you back from the abyss as weak minded and foolish. Their faith is their shame yet they wear it proudly. How could they? Have they no independent thought? ... no self-worth? ...no inward motivation?

You grieve alone. Sure, you have friends but you can't find peace. There's nothing to replace the loss you feel. It happens to everyone eventually... some sooner than others. You're not sweating the small stuff.

You have no hope beyond this life. Your only hope is that you're right about all of it...that your purpose is limited to a mere 80 years of showing the world what you've got...Then nothing... You're suddenly 70...too late to reconsider...or so you think.

You deny even a glimpse of God in creation. It's all just something you refer to as wonder. There's a scientific explanation for everything and science is never wrong. It's always operator error.

You will wither and turn back to dust. In your mind, there's nothing beyond the last date on your headstone...It's all about what you accomplish in the "dash between the dates." You'll create a better world on your own.

You pity the foolish because they rely on an invisible God...yet your wisdom dissolves in truth... You can't imagine why they are so happy...these ignorant do-gooders that grovel before their perfect God...these readers of an ancient book that keeps them bound... these prayerful, helpful vestiges of a long, deceptive culture...these followers of Jesus Christ known only for His suffering and ultimate death. You can't imagine that they believe He did it for them. What must they be thinking?

Then you read this...

> *Psalm 14:1*
> *"The fool hath said in his heart, there is no God. They are corrupt, they have done abominable works, there is none that doeth good."*

and you start to wonder if you've beaten back the only thing that can save you from yourself...

What if this is true?

> *Colossians 1:15-17*
> *The Son is the image of the invisible God, the firstborn over all creation. For in him all things were created: things in heaven and on earth, visible and invisible, whether thrones or powers or rulers or authorities; all things have been created through him and for him. He is before all things, and in him all things hold together.*

Moving Day

WHEN HE FIRST handed it to her, she didn't know how to hold it... so she just clutched it to her chest and let the corner brush away the tears on her face. She held back the sobs. She had to... She was the strong one now...She had to remember the kids...They needed to see what she was made of. They needed to know she was up to the task.

She walked away from the grave holding both their hands., She stopped and thanked Sgt. Baker. He hugged the kids. She let little Tommy hold it because he'd asked if he could and he needed something of his dad's right now.

She knew that somehow all her anguish needed to turn to courage. Dear God, how? she wondered. She remembered the Bible verse he read to her. It was the one he took on patrol...the one he'd copied onto the back of the photo of her and the kids. They found it in his lifeless hand, bloodied from the skirmish. "Do not fear: I am with you; do not be anxious: I am your God. I will strengthen you; I will help you; I will uphold you with my victorious right hand. " She repeated it over and over. Those words calmed her more than anything. She could almost hear Tom's voice as he read them to her.

She'd have to lose that feeling that came over her at times... that he was coming back... that he was just doing his job and he'd be home soon. He always came home. That's what he did. Besides... he promised. How could he not?

Back home she busied herself. She started to pack. When she got to the medicine cabinet, she opened the bottle and smelled his aftershave again... just to remember... just to be with him...The days without him were too long.

Sometimes she'd sit in "his" chair in the living room and stare at the wooden frame on the mantle...She really needed to take it out and get that little bit of makeup off of it...It didn't seem right... Maybe she would soon but she knew when she did, the memories would swarm her.

She'd start to remember the look in that soldier's eyes when he presented it to her...the way he looked deep into her soul and thanked her. She knew he meant it. He'd had to say it far too many times. His stare was fixed but there was certain despair in the almost chiseled wrinkles already forming in his young face. He was battle hardened. Just like Tom. That's when the rush would come... That's when the shadow moved across her heart. That's when she would bite her lip to hold back the sobs... The kids couldn't hear that. They'd be up soon. She could almost hear, "Suck it up, cupcake."...Tom's favorite command.

This was one of those mornings when the pain was just too much. She'd have to go about the business of making the kid's breakfast soon. She would hear reveille one last time. This was their last day on base. They'd be moving back to mom's house today...

She couldn't bear the thought of leaving. They'd been here nearly two years through both deployments. The other wives had been amazing since the funeral... but she knew she reminded them that their husbands could be next. It was time to go.

She still didn't know how to carry it...even in the frame. It was a triangle and a bit awkward. She'd take it with her in the car. Mom would know what to do. They'd cry together first then they'd go about the business of getting the kids settled. They needed the attention.

It would go on the shelf next to Dad's and Uncle Pete's in the family room...Yet another sentry guarding them, keeping watch in the night...daring any intruder to cross. That thought gave her comfort somehow even though she knew it wasn't really true.

After all.... It was only a flag...

In Defense of Baptists

I've been to a lot of Baptist churches in my life. The only thing ever crammed down my throat was Miss Beauchamp's fried chicken, some mashed taters and gravy...and a tub o' her homemade nanner puddin' of course.

The only "bible thumping" I can remember was back when there weren't no air conditionin'...so we left the windows open and we killed 'skeeters with whatever was close...and a hard cover bible was always in the pew in front of us...so thumpin' was perty common.

We had two men git married once...and they still are...It was what they called a "double wedding." Their brides was there too...They had kids later on...Nobody hated nobody. I don't know what all the fuss is about two men gittin' married.

We dunk people. That's what we do when they come to Jesus. Nobody has ever drowned, though some squirm more than others. (My daddy says that the reason Presbyterian churches are so big is 'cause they save so much money on the water bill). but to us... sprinklin' only works on maters.

No matter what the signs say...God don't call nobody "fag"...He calls us "sinners" and "children"...and God don't hate nobody... He ain't necessarily proud of all of us, but he don't hate nobody!

Them people protestin' at the funerals ain't none of us. They're like an adopted Uncle. God loves 'em but nobody misses 'em at reunions...'cause their invitation always ends up in that drawer nobody looks in... We cain't tell you what bible they're readin' but it ain't the good book!

We believe the bible. Every word of it...We don't believe God would give us a bad book so's we'd have to figger out which parts was good and which weren't. We think perty highly of God... When everything else is bad. He's right there with us...stickin' to us like lightnin bug sweat. (If you don't know what that is you're probly a Yankee. God loves you too...We try to...but God ain't finished with us yet!)

We don't take our guns to church...Yeah...You go ahead and believe that but you touch one of our kids while they're there, and the next sound you hear will be what we like to call the "holy clicks of righteousness." What follows is called "crickets." That's just how it is.

We love Jesus because he loved us first. He loved us so much, he died on the cross for us. and yes!...We believe he rose again!... Nothin' says he didn't 'ceptin people who believe in aliens and unicorns and such. We know he did 'cause we talk with him all the time!

And just so you know...We love everybody...and all that talk about snake handlin' and stuff...Naw...Uh Uh...We don't know those people either...Bless their hearts...but you cain't fix stupid...

The best way to git to know us is for y'all to come see us!...That Jesus you don't believe in will be there! You can talk to him yerself!...We'll interduce you...It's what we do!

Just know that everbody that calls themselves "Baptists" ain't... any more than people who call themselves lawyers or bankers... or politishuns...Just 'cause they say they are, don't make them proper representatives...

The bible says, "Ye shall know them by their fruits"...So, come have some apple pie and some of' Miss Beauchamp's nanner puddin...I think you'll take a differnt view of what a Baptist is.... We'll teach you how to say, "Bless yo' heart" to the meanest people you know!

I Beat...

YOU CAN HEAR me if you listen closely...I'm a steady, barely audible thumping inside your chest. I am central to your existence. I am the muscle that sustains you. I cause you to "be."

My main purpose is to beat, to pump, to distribute life sustaining blood throughout the body. I am deliberate and built specifically for the job.

I don't know where this purpose originates...I only know that there is an Originator, otherwise how could I exist...or function at all?

I provide lifeblood to all the other parts. If I fail to beat, I too, cease to exist.

I can feel. I am the place where emotions reside... I am the center of life...Without me, life ceases.

I'm not sure why exertion causes me to pound harder or why relaxation slows me down...I don't know why stress affects me or why I am saddened when another heart stops pumping. I am not a reasoning organ.

But I do hear a voice...It keeps me beating...It is constant and sure. It is not the voice of my host or the voice of those other, confusing voices...It is the voice of my Maker...He speaks to me and makes every beat possible. He alone controls my rhythm, my speed, my longevity.

I do as He commands...If I am told to slow down, I will slow down...If I am told to race, I will race... If I am told to cease, I will cease...I have no sense of self. I am solely dependent on my Maker's commands.

If I fail to hear Him or cease to follow His commands, I begin to hate...and I can hate with a vengeance. I can hate until I harden. I can affect the other parts and cause pain...I can despise. I can loathe. I can hate so deeply that I will cease to listen to my Maker's voice. I stagnate without His direction.

Sometimes I break...not in a mechanical way but in a moment of pain or loss, I am disturbed and desperate. I can become sorrowful and forlorn. I can grieve, sometimes for a lifetime.

But oh, how I can love! My Maker touches me and speaks to me in a way that causes me to beat to His command. We are connected, perfectly synchronized. That is when I can connect with other hearts and feel their presence...I am joyous when I love. I am perpetual, eternal, I am one with my Maker.

When I love, I cause the other parts to dance and sing and laugh. That is when I am at my best...That is when the rhythm is perfected. That is when I realize that I am His and He has purposed me not just to beat...but to love... because He first loved me.

That is when I know that I am fearfully and wonderfully made... and whose name is inscribed on my very walls.

> ~ Proverbs 4:23
> "Above all else, guard your heart, for everything you do flows from it."

Forgive Us Our Trespasses

IF IT'S ALL true... If God is who he says he is...If the simplest of bible truths are profound... then I have a reason to confront you with the truth. That is my job...my first command...the focal point of my life.

The Christian journey is...by all accounts, an attempt to take others with us to the place we know as heaven. We have specific instructions from the one to whom we submit our lives... to love you... and to introduce you to the one who died for us and went to prepare a place for us.

We realize your reticence to believe us. We know it takes Jesus himself, to intervene and stir within you a desire to follow him... but our job is still the same...to love you...and make every attempt to introduce you to the God of heaven.

Yes, we seek your friendship...Yes, we want you to know the peace we know...Yes, we want to honor God by being an example to you...Yes many of us are poor examples...Yes many of us find it difficult to make the introduction without appearing judgmental. Yes...Many are at different stages of Christian growth and tend to be over zealous...Yes...Sometimes we just make a mess of it...

But know this...God has put us in front of you for a reason. In this way, we are a testament to his existence, his love and his desire to be involved with those who don't know him. It is his love we wish to share...a love so great that it is beyond even our own human ability to express it.

-John 13:34
"A new command I give you: Love one another. As I have loved you, so you must love one another."

Lakeside Theater

So...No TV here at Lake Takeabreath...Still, much drama... Osprey and eagle fight...not many torn feathers...just a lot of screeching...Apparently, someone got a fish...I always like to look at the fish as he flies away in the eagles clutches because the look on his face is hilarious...kindalike..."Hey look!..I'm fly-yyyiiiiing..."...Then an "Uh Oh" moment...

A frog sucked a spider off the screen faster than I really expected he could...Would like to see that in slow-motion... That's how I want to go...just *SCHLAP*...Hello Jesus!

The most dramatic episode was when a possum the size of a freakin' Shetland pony decided to come out from under the deck just as the sun went down. He walked across the sea wall like that's what he's supposed to do...He looked at me...I know he did... but he didn't say anything so I guess we're cool...I started to shoot him but he scampered back before I could actually open the door.. (my wife hates for me to shoot through the screen.)

There're more bugs out here than I even want to think about... There's bugs so big they trip you so the rest can feed. You can hear them buzzing, lurking...waiting for to gnaw on some human flesh. All those diseases they carry have to go somewhere...

I can't begin to explain what's happening in that water... Something's eatin' something and whatever it is will be breakfast for the gators...They eat what they want to eat...when they want to eat it. They're kinda like lions in the lake...Kings of the water.

It don't really matter if it's above the water or below. Those dudes will eat it!

Apparently, something is in season. Every once in a while, somebody fires off about thirty rounds. They're either a bad shot or mad about something.

It's about time for the frog symphony so I have to get to my seat on the porch for that...Watching the solar dock lights come on is pretty cool as well...one at a time...I always try to guess which one is next...I don't know why...

It's like a soap opera here...Once you're wrapped up in it, you look forward to the next episode...The next one will involve a sunrise... Always worth getting up to watch... Stay tuned!

How to MRI

ONCE YOU'RE IN the tube, let the fun begin...

Minute 1: "Bridge to engine room...DIVE...DIVE!"
<make annoying buzzer sounds as you go into the tube>

Minute 3: "Tower, this is Maverick requesting a flyby."<make loud annoying radio noise>

Minute 5: <Make beat box sounds to irritate the nurses>...
"Now, this is a story all about how
My life got flipped-turned upside down
And I'd like to take a minute
Just sit right there
I'll tell you how I became the prince of a town called Bel Air..."

Minute 8: <singing> "96 bottles of beer on the wall...96 bottles of beeeer! Take one down...pass it around...95 bottles of beer on the wall...95 bottles" (ad infinitum)

Minute 12: <SING LOUD!>

"Ground Control to Major Tom
Your circuit's dead,
there's something wrong
Can you hear me, Major Tom?
Can you hear me, Major Tom?
Can you hear me, Major Tom?
Can you..."

Heeeeere am I floating
round my tin can
Faaaar above the Moon
Planet Earth is blue
And there's nothing I can do."

Minute 15..." What if I have one of those aliens that pop out of my stomach? There's no room for him..."

No answer...

Minute 16: PUNCH...PUNCH...PUNCH!...
MUST..." KILL...BILL..." PUNCH...
PUNCH!

Minute 17...<sound serious>" They're cloning me...I just know it...If I get outta' here and there's two of me...I'm gonna kill it... Just know that!"

Minute 18: "Get us out of here, Sulu...Warp 9...ENGAGE!"

Minute 19...<Sing again...louder>
"We gotta get outta this plaaace...if it's the last thing we eveer dooo!"

Minute 20: and this is hilarious but the nurses were pretty sick of me by the time I was on my way out...

"It's...It's a BOY...IT'S A BEAUTIFUL BOY, MRS. WALTON... We'll call him John...John boy Walton...but wait...Is that a mole? ...NOOOOOOOOOOO!"

Then I acted as if nothing had happened.

Disciplan

WHEN I WAS in Basic Training (Infantry, Ft. Benning, Ga. HOOAH!) I contracted the German measles...It was kind of cool to watch my Drill Sergeant freak completely out when I pulled my shirt up in formation and showed him my red splattered torso...It was the only time I had seen him NOT maintain calm under pressure. After all, this was the man trained to pick up a live grenade and toss it out of the box in the event that someone accidentally dropped a live one.

I was immediately sequestered and sent to Martin Army Hospital. I think I was there a total of five days. I remember that it was an upper respiratory illness and that I was pretty sick for most of that time...I also remember my former girlfriend calling to see how I was and casually telling me about her new boyfriend... UNGH! Miserable doesn't quite describe my world during that time.

I was ordered to get up and walk around every day...Not many folks came in to check on me due to the risk of exposure...but they did issue orders from outside the door. I remember the awful experience of having to shine my boots each morning and dress in the proper uniform when I wasn't in bed. I couldn't imagine how keeping a sharp uniform appearance could possibly be helpful in my recovery...but I did recover just in time for a required bivouac in sub-freezing temperatures...I still graduated with my cycle. Kinda' proud of that!

In hindsight, I realize that I was being taught that maintaining discipline was still important. I was still learning to be a soldier... learning also that the rules didn't change just because I wasn't feeling well. Doctors were still officers to be obeyed. and I was still way down on the list of decision makers. What seemed foolish then, actually taught me a lesson I've never forgotten... Maintain discipline even in the midst of turmoil. Do what is directly in front of you...and listen for instructions.

You never know what God has in store for you. Read the bible and pray...no matter what...It's like putting on a fresh uniform and shiny boots...You may feel like you've been sucker punched...but at least you're presentable.

> *"For whom the LORD loves he corrects; even as a father the son in whom he delights."*
> -Proverbs 3:12

Pavlov's Bible

RATHER THAN VIEW a sunrise or otherwise engage in the phenomenon that is a new day, we reach for our dinging phones and punch in what passes for the daily news. We begin the process of keeping our heads on a swivel, constantly shaking it back and forth as we read the incredulous accounts of what the political machines and complicit editors have decided we will argue about today.

We have all but forgotten the book that once brought hope to a dying world. We have all but dismissed the main character who suffered and died so that we might live. We have relegated Him to history rather than to enjoy His presence. We have forgotten His charge to love God and to love one another.

We have instead, been numbed to the point of starting our days reading about which politician, sports figure, Hollywood celebrity or other malcontent has been selected by the media to be our sworn enemy today.

Conversely, our assigned guardian angel hero's response will give us all the hope we need because they're out there "fighting for us." Our phones ding with every notification from our imaginary friends. Thumbs up, we agree to agree.

We could begin to read the actual, infallible, inspired words of a holy and righteous God...but we'd rather not. We'd rather be participants in the right vs. left affray, or the religious squabbles or some invented racial strife or even a new, formatted agenda flush with flags and slogans...all demanding rights and adherence to some ambiguous moral tenet, suddenly discovered by an ethereal sounding mouthpiece.

We enjoy the contentious world and accept the foul influences in our own lives. We have no real source of power.

We are but automatons existing in a barrage of digitally created opinions, selecting our own conclusions from a list of preordained and grossly manipulated ideas presented to us in a multiple-choice format.

The people who control our morning know that. They know that we are just trained, expectant, yapping puppies running to our respective bowls of canned mystery meat dujour, gulping down the contents as soon as we hear the ding that notifies us of a new entry into our list of important subjects by our trusted friends. We rush to gain entrance into the "real world." Only it isn't.

We literally await the 4 o'clock bell that signals it's okay to buy that new car or boat even a house we can't afford in the imminent economic downturn.

We feel engaged and motivated to adjust our diet, our blood pressure, our cholesterol...whatever the web doctors tell us.

We've forgotten the source of truth...We've evolved to a place of multiple truths. Everyone has their own truth, their own virtue, their own worldview, their own lifestyle...and we wonder why we are divided.

But here lies the truth, buried forever in the dust pile of leather-bound books of antiquity. It's as easy as punching in the words

"Holy Bible" but we detest the idea of accepting His book as truth. We discount it because we're told it contains no truth. We accept that it was written by mere men under no inspiration from God. We accept that because we are short on things to believe in.

We have become literally hopeless. We expect the gift of tomorrow rather than to put our trust in the Maker of today. We listen for the bell that will call us to prayer, or forgiveness, or *gasp* repentance.

I am suddenly and profoundly aware of the hopelessness in the world. I believe that thought alone has led me to pick up my copy of the word of God and seek Divine wisdom rather than to search the endless abyss of media for direction.

I pray that you too will make that choice. Indeed, there is hope beyond the screen, beyond the chatter, beyond the protests.

Jesus is who He says He is. His is the name above every other name. He said of Himself, "All authority in heaven and on earth has been given to me."

If that means nothing to you, I'd appeal to you to at least read about Him...Don't let others decide your eternal future.

> *Hebrews 4:12*
> *"For the word of God is quick, and powerful, and sharper than any two-edged sword, piercing even to the dividing asunder of soul and spirit, and of the joints and marrow, and is a discerner of the thoughts and intentions of the heart.*

Wordlessness

I KEEP READING ABOUT the increase in people taking their own lives...It seems to be escalating and while I don't necessarily want to dwell on the subject, I am overwhelmed by the numbers and drawn to encourage folks with "the hope that lies within me."

It is clear that people have no hope beyond themselves. There's wisdom in that thought... and potential failure. We are built to enjoy a relationship with our Creator. When we don't enjoy that relationship, we are bound to feel alone. There's no place to put our loneliness, our grief, our sadness. People who don't believe such things or rule them out completely, live in a place of self-dependency. When they run out of self, and they will, there's nothing to grab on to. There's no weapon, no defense against the world, no drug, no answer, no hope. That is the long and short of it. People run out of hope.

I believe that is because we have moved away from our only strength. We've lost the words we need to sustain ourselves because they're not just words. They're words from the very One who created us. They are words that give us strength and hope. They are words that affect the very core of our being, our soul, our reason for existing...eternal truths that get buried into our hearts... burned into our minds... Words that carry us through to tomorrow past our seemingly inescapable today.

Rejecting the words, the words of God, is to reject the hope they bring. The Bible is the revelation, the revealing of Jesus Christ who came to bring us hope, who died for our transgressions as an expression of love and who continues to invite us to trust and depend on Him. He is the source of hope... the strength we need in times of trouble.

Share these verses with a friend. Reach out to folks who may be beyond themselves and in search of a way to move forward. Pray for them and have an eternal conversation with them. It may be all they need to get through the day... and into a relationship with the only hope that any of us really have.

> *Psalm: 40:1*
> *"I waited patiently for the LORD; he turned to me and heard my cry. He lifted me out of the slimy pit, out of the mud and mire; he set my feet on a rock and gave me a firm place to stand. He put a new song in my mouth, a hymn of praise to our God. Many will see and fear the LORD and put their trust in him.*
>
> *1Peter 5:6,7*
> *"Humble yourselves, therefore, under God's mighty hand, that he may lift you up in due time. Cast all your anxiety on him because he cares for you."*
> *-1 Peter 5:6-7*

Beach Front

WHENEVER I SEE a photo of the Normandy landing, I put myself on that Amphibious Assault Vehicle and I wonder what my prayer would have been...and how I would go about the business of focusing my attention on the mission with so much death in front of me...Of course it's only imagination...but still I wonder...

Imagine the guts it took to storm that beach with the guys in front of you being slaughtered like cattle...some still floating in the water...the ocean churning up the blood and spilling it onto the beach...

The first wave has already been decimated... then the second... Many are pinned down...You can't hear commands over all the explosions...You can feel the concussion from every shell... the sand blasts the vehicle...The sky is dark from smoke...Then you're up!...

How do you explain that kind of fortitude?...that kind of courage?... that sense of devotion to a cause?...Those who stood "between us and them" should never be regarded as anything but an example to the rest of us...not just a memory, rather a motivation...to do better...to be courageous in the face of adversity...to stand in the gap!...To run toward the fire!

Remember these when you see the American flag being burned... or when you hear the droning voices that despise this America... Know that these men...these courageous souls... refused to accept the tyranny that spread like wildfire across an unsuspecting world. They weren't just soldiers...They were America!

Know that this "day at the beach" was one of the many days these American souls endured. Honor them…and don't let anyone tell you "who we are" without considering them!

Know that deep down in the soul of America these men still exist. Thank Almighty God that they do…Pray for them! Lift them up to the Throne of Grace because they do what others will not…They keep coming…They run toward the fire!

Book Sales

MANY YEARS AGO, I was taught a basic principle of sales...It went something like this. "It's not really necessary to put down a competitor's product if yours is good enough to stand on its own." That basically means that the features and benefits (merits) of your product, should be enough for it to stand alone in the marketplace.

In today's marketplace of ideas , it seems there is so much "anti-everything," there's just no room for positivity...It's kind of strange how people will openly state what is wrong with your beliefs... but rarely report what it is they believe because they would risk the same scrutiny...Somehow they believe their science book dismisses any teaching from the bible...as if it is a "science vs. bible" world...or...If you believe the bible is true, then that automatically means that you are "anti-science, "as if one cannot understand science because it doesn't promote biblical understanding.

We could, by virtue of the many failed efforts of the sciences, point directly at those failures and their associated books as a method of promoting our own belief. But that isn't any way to promote the truth... because the truth will stand on its own. The bible tells us to "Contend for the faith"...not to be contentious. (As I write this, I realize what Paul must have felt when he referred to himself as "Chief sinner")

With that in mind, Christians everywhere should stand on the bible as the inerrant word of God. It isn't necessary to put down other religious views or even deride the misinterpretation of those who try to use it as a weapon against what is or isn't "acceptable" social behavior. Those who are "anti" bible will always exist. The futility of their efforts is shown in the fact that the bible still exists and can still be used as THE long term, reliable source for moral direction...The bible retains its eternal value no matter the current social behaviors.

The bible is the revelation (revealing) of Jesus Christ... The Son of God, who came to save the world. He died on a cross so that all might live, and rose again on the third day. He is now seated at the right hand of the Father. We will all meet him, someday. That is the story. There is no greater truth!

What the bible isn't, is a comic book with a Super hero character. Those who are "anti-bible" generally have so little understanding of it, they tend to compare it with what they know...myths, fairy tales, science fiction,...Realizing that these are their comparative examples provides us with an opportunity...one that allows us to distinguish our story from those based on fantasy. Superman may protect you...but he doesn't offer you eternal life.

Ours is to study the bible and apply it to our lives so that we will be proper and dignified ambassadors...pointing always to our perfect King, Jesus Christ!... holding high the Word of God because it stands alone atop all other books. There is no other book that compares...

and here is why...

> *"All scripture is given by inspiration of God, and is profitable for doctrine, for reproof, for correction, for instruction in righteousness:"*
> 2 Timothy 3:16

Salt and Light Version.

I STRUCK UP A casual conversation this morning with an elderly man at a local breakfast restaurant. He'd hung his cane on a chair behind the only available seating. He tried to move it so I could get by him. I motioned that it wasn't in my way.

We talked for a few minutes. One thing led to another and I casually quoted a bible verse, which is kinda' my way if I have the opportunity.

He responded with "People don't read the Bible anymore."...

I responded with, "Quick...Tell me all the good things that are going on in the world today!"... Really long pause...so I bought his breakfast and told him, "I read it this morning!"

You may be the only bible some people ever read. Try to be a good translation.

> Matthew 5:13-16
> "You are the salt of the earth, but if salt has lost its taste, how can its saltiness be restored? It is no longer good for anything except to be trampled under people's feet. "You are the light of the world. A city set on a hill cannot be hidden. Nor do people light a lamp and put it under a basket, but on a stand, and it gives light to all in the house. In the same way, let your light shine before others, so that they may see your good works and give glory to your Father who is in heaven.

Dock of Ages

IT EXTENDS OUT 360 feet from shore... which equals the same number of degrees I can see on a plane, from its end. It was far too expensive to build but necessary in order to span the eel grass. Eel grass is the perfect environment for breeding fish and other aquatic life. Hence the need to span it. The sandy bottoms here make it the perfect place for any number of species to bed...So it is a good thing to span the grass even if it did require two additions and became the longest dock on Crescent Lake. We didn't intend to build it that long but "rules is rules" so we did what we had to do.

My grandfather is "buried" there at the end of it. A couple of fisherman friends and myself emptied his urn into the slight wind and watched some of his ashes swirl out over the lake...the rest sinking and taking off in the current. "Daddy Harold" was the embodiment of the storied, Southern fisherman. He would have loved that exit. It was reverent and prayerful. Of course, it wasn't actually him. He's in heaven. It was what many call his "remains" but I take issue with that. He was so much a part of who I turned out to be that I consider myself his remains.

My dad is out on the end of the dock as well. He was buried in Atlanta. I spoke at his funeral in South Georgia but was unable to make the drive to witness his interment. After the service, I drove what seemed a million miles to our lake house to gather my thoughts before returning home. I grabbed a fishing pole and made the trek out to the end of the dock. If you knew my dad, you'd know that was the right thing to do. I climbed over into the boat hanging from the sling. I just stared at the water and wished my dad was there. He was never able to make the trip to see the house or the dock... but I knew he could see them now, through the eyes of his "remains." I remembered the hymns we sang at his funeral. I sang them out there, to God Himself, through tears only sons can shed at the loss of their father... In doing so, I went from a place of grief to a place only God can produce...a place where recovery is possible, where pain turns to indelible memory. The Scriptures refer to that place as the "peace beyond understanding."

I made several trips out to the end of the dock that weekend we lost my dad, all with the same intent... to mentally lay a wreath of remembrance and decide what and who I was going to be from that point forward...not to erase their memory, rather to decide on the best way to fill the shoes of those who had come before me. I had to work out how I would be that man they prayed I would become. I am after all, what remains of great men who loved the Lord. This was the place I began to "work out my own salvation" (Philippians 2:12-13,)

My thoughts always go to family when I'm out on the dock...particularly those who have gone to be with the Lord. We recently had a visit with some of my family and watched as they too enjoyed the view... and the fishing...and the reminiscing. It was great to see them experience it for the first time. I'm sure they realized that they were all remains as well. The dock has a sobering effect.

My wife loves to fish out at the end. I'm not out there as much as she is. She too is an avid fisherman. There is literally nothing in my life that compares to watching her haul in a big one. She doesn't know this but the laugh she lets out is identical to the one she made the day I proposed to her...It is filled with a conquering, almost gloating tone. It is her Viking laugh... I guess she reserves it for her bigger catches...<insert muffled laughter>

I could go on about the dock. It has healing properties in more ways than you might imagine...It is a place to collect ourselves, to remember those who came before us and a place to align ourselves with the one who created us. At night, you can see forever from there.

So, thank you Lord for this, our dock. Thank you for this view of the Eastern sky where we can stand and watch another sunrise in anticipation of your return. Thank you for the view that shouts of an eternity beyond our imaginations. Thank you for all the great times we share on this narrow boardwalk...this path to peace...this place of remembrance. Thank you for all the reflection it sparks and the way you point to yourself in all of nature. We are humbled in your presence. We acknowledge your grace and mercy extended to us, your servants. We are thankful for each of your gifts and for your boundless love.

It is well with my soul.

> *Revelation. 21:4*
> *'He will wipe every tear from their eyes. There will be no more death' or mourning or crying or pain, for the old order of things has passed away."*

Complaint Deportment

WE'VE FORGOTTEN WHO we really are... Instead of counting our blessings we've reversed our outlook and found a way to complain about virtually everything. We have come to a place as a nation where we literally cannot see the blessings of the forest for the problematic trees.

Watching the 24/7 news is now an exercise in just how futile the fight to survive has become, not to mention that we seek answers from media "panels of experts" who literally expose American dirty laundry as if they have become the moral standard by which we all must measure ourselves.

Our days are spent listening to never ending complaints about inequality and injustice and the burdens of life itself, as if protest and whining will cure those ailments.

Seemingly ignorant of our own manipulation, we stand under a blood-soaked flag that offers more opportunity than any other piece of geography in the world. The privilege we have, that we all have, is part of our heritage. It was bought and paid for by people who saw the vision we no longer share.

Mankind will not suddenly become humane and understanding of one another. There is no end to the evil and corruption. We are each identified as either the oppressed or the oppressor, with no actual solution to that predicament. Where then, is hope?

If you're reading this, God hasn't moved. He still maintains control over the universe...everything from the weather to the axis on which this globe spins. That's not going to change whether you personally believe He exists or not. Our hope and our future lie there. It always has.

Our opportunity doesn't lie in the hands of government or the ideas of a complicit media. They want us miserable because they lust after one thing...Our vote!

Our opportunity was provided to us by courageous men and women who still serve at the expense of their own freedom. They choose to defend. They are vital to our spirit. They remain vigilant. Thank God for each of them!

This America remains under the protection of a mighty God. He decides what is just and unjust. He resolves complaint and creates the path forward. He doesn't seek your vote. He appoints kings and has dominion over world affairs. He alone can solve the problems inherent in our system of government.

What America (dare I say Americans) should once again pursue is their own communal happiness that rests beyond the malcontented complaint and manufactured controversy...

We should once again look to the very heavens. There are no panels of experts there...only the One who died so that we might be free, indeed. He is seated at the right hand of the Father. He is the God of mercy and love and protection for the weak. He is the very source of our strength. He alone avenges the cruelty, the injustice, the hateful acts of men who seek to harm other men.

In this America, we are all still free to worship Him... We all still have the privilege of knowing Him... We all still have the opportunity to meet and share in the promise of an eternity with Him.

That is the blessing. That is the wealth of America. It's not in the never-ending complaint or the corrupted man exposed by other corrupted men. That is theater maintained by those who profit from the exposure while hiding their own corruption.

Our countenance has become one of despair. The world sees us as dominated by a lack of hope. We have become ingrates and malcontents in a country flush with blessing and opportunity brought to us by those who came before us. We are limited only by our own vision of the future. We have allowed ourselves to be swayed by profiteers who are themselves corrupted.

It's time to raise our voices to heaven and look beyond the crippling effects of an out of control and ever-present drone of complaint. We must once again touch our knees to the altar of blessing and seek guidance from the only measure of truth that still exists.

God shed His grace on Thee!

> *1 Chronicles 29:11*
> *O Lord, you are great, mighty, majestic, magnificent, glorious, and sovereign over all the sky and earth! You have dominion and exalt yourself as the ruler of all.*

United Stakes

I AM PRIVILEGED BECAUSE I am an American...or at least I was once privileged. I guess the term "proud American" is a bit old fashioned at this point. Still, I was afforded great opportunity throughout my life, not just by geography but by divine blessing.

I was born a free man with all the opportunities set forth by a Constitution written by dutiful, free men following their corporate "Declaration of Independence" from the tyranny that had beset them. Each of them may as well have signed in blood as their very lives were given for the cause we have obviously forgotten

These, our forefathers, were the first of many to whom I am personally indebted for the privilege of living the majority of my life under a semblance of freedom...but I always knew that it was defended and preserved with blood on battlefields throughout the world. I always knew of the sacrifice of those who came before me. I revered them as did everyone I knew, as I remember. We all pledged allegiance.

Clearly, many younger Americans no longer hold certain "truths to be self-evident"...because they have never been taught to revere their predecessors. They do not regard gratitude as a viable trait... They do not revere any American enterprise nor do they see Americans as exceptional.

They only understand history as it is interpreted by malcontents. They believe wealth is only gained through greed and power through dissent. They honor nothing except their own omnidirectional sense of right and wrong.

They believe that America has never been great, or above the fray, or good in any way. Indeed, they believe that God has neither blessed nor preserved America...because God doesn't exist and America is a hellish pit of inequality and injustice.

Yet, they insist that they have rights without understanding where they come from or the need to defend them. They live under the flag of moral equivalence and consider their discontent a righteous cause...a cause by which they can gain more from the wealthy producers if they just demand it.

If we have failed at all, it is in that place...to have not taught the young the value of their freedom...to not point to the higher authority that guides this America...to have sat idly by and allowed our children to be taught irreverence and disdain for the very ones to whom freedom was taken, in the hopes that their lifeblood would be a fair trade for the freedom of those who would follow them...their children and their children's children.

It begins with the documents. Our rights are indeed "endowed by our Creator." If we have evolved beyond any reverence for that Creator, we must look to a new source for these rights that so many adamantly demand...or we must hand them over to a more benevolent benefactor.

Who might that be? Who provides the freedom of dissent? Who defends the poor and feeds the hungry? Who can we trust to right the wrongs? Who holds mercy or justice or equality in the palm of their hand?

It appears as though freedom is now decided by the those who seek to destroy it. There is a new breed of American...one that views a new, revised history...one that seeks oppression...one that doesn't fight against tyranny, rather it invites it as a new version of what America "ought to be." They hold to the dark side of history rather than to rise above her growing pains. They are stuck in the mire demanding acknowledgement of the sins perpetrated by their oppressors rather than to seek favor from the only place of blessing...or to be grateful for all of our deliverance from evil.

Not only do they kneel at the very symbol of that freedom and blessing, they demand that others abide it...those who have experienced the loss of a friend or family member...those who have defended that banner against evil so that others will never have to fear again.

Their complicit puppet masters train their cameras on the protests rather than honor the banner under which their freedom was secured. They believe their irreverence for the symbol of freedom somehow promotes a cause...one they insist is borne of righteous demands against an ever present and calculated cruelty, rather than the sinful nature of all men.

I am of this mind, though I abhor the thought of watching the upheaval, that it may be time to allow them their fight. Perhaps it is time to end the experiment and accept that men cannot govern themselves...that this America was never worth fighting for, that the blood was all in vain...every drop of it spilled for nothing more than vain obsession.Perhaps we should learn again the terrible lesson of the loss of freedom so that we might once again consider the One who "giveth and taketh away."

This civil war they propose may be the blessing of a righteous and just God, the winner being decided at the outset in heaven itself.

Perhaps then, the phrase "God and Country" will once again be a viable threat and truth will prevail against the evils that have once again come against her...this writhing flailing, hateful America.

Or...

We can all stand up as that banner passes and offer the respect due those who gave their lives for it...

Then we can kneel together before a mighty and loving God who loves us and has bestowed countless blessings on every single one of us. We...Americans!

Standing up as the banner yet waves is the perfect depiction of the real cause of unity. To do otherwise is a signal to the world that we are open to their destructive efforts.

God Bless America!

Sing Louder! Pray harder! Love Deeper!

> *Romans 12:18,*
> *"If it is possible, as far as it depends on you, live at peace with everyone.*

A Back-Yard Fable

MY WIFE AND I watched the turtle slowly make its way up from the canal. She began to lay her eggs in the dirt by the fence. She methodically covered each of them to hide them from whatever might do them harm. The coconut tree offered some shade when it was still, so keeping the eggs somewhat cool must have been her effort.

Enter the crow! He was big and intimidating and overly aggressive. He didn't have to show his swag. He was bigger and stronger. He pecked the turtleress (Shuddup, I make my own words sometimes.) on the shell while she was still laying the eggs. He pecked hard on a couple of the eggs and broke them. He ate a bit of the yolk(s), making a show of it and perched himself back on the fence, anticipating more food.

We watched the crime as it was being committed and decided to get involved. (No, I couldn't shoot the crow. Here in suburbia, that would be akin to handcuffing myself to a water tower and shooting the neighbor's dogs)

As I was readying myself to go out, a couple of brave (and loud) mockingbirds showed up and started dive bombing the crow, pecking and punishing him for every move toward the eggs...not to mention all of the bird-cursing they did in the process. I don't speak bird but I could understand every shrill chirp in between the wing flapping. They were ruthless! The crow still tried to get more eggs but the mockingbirds forced him to defend himself.

Just as it looked like the battle would be lost, it rained... It rained hard! The rain pelted the battlefield and scattered the combatants. There was suddenly calm...like when the oars come out of the water and you hear absolutely nothing...That kinda' calm.

The turtle headed back down to the canal, looking a bit tired from the battle and somewhat sad from the loss of two of her own. (like I can read the expression on a turtle's face when she's walking away...Shuddup...It's my story)

Several morals to the story came to mind, no single one would cover the entire event. Too many actors...So here's what I gained from the fracas...I'm sharing this with you because you read this far so you deserve some kind of reward...

Be a turtle! Do what you gotta do! There's plenty of time. There's gonna be battles! But you'll get through it. There may be some losses, but it's a journey. Do the best you can and move on!

Don't be a freakin' crow...It ain't all about you!... Yeah, you gotta eat but not at the expense of others. Don't take just because you can. Learn some manners. They're good to have when you get old.

Be courageous! Carry yourself like a mockingbird. When you see something that just ain't right, DO something! Defend those who can't defend themselves! Sometimes it takes more than one mockingbird to help others.

Lastly, God's got this! In the end, it was the rain that brought peace to the whole situation. He controls that as well. We're all so quick to jump in and fix things. God doesn't necessarily need our help. He needs our attention...and our obedience!

And of course, a Bible verse which changes the whole idea of a fable to an actual devotional of sorts.

> *Matthew 5:45*
> *"That ye may be the children of your Father which is in heaven: for he makes his sun to rise on the evil and on the good, and sends rain on the just and on the unjust."*

Sin-full

...OR...

How to lose friends by discussing the inevitability of consequences.

Sin travels at terrific speeds...It reproduces itself exponentially without any foreseeable end. Even the mention of it has become taboo, as if by not discussing it, we will somehow become immune to its power...Out of sight = out of mind ya' know.

In my own life I can attest to watching the speed at which mankind has spiraled toward depravity while intuitively being in awe of it. I've watched as we've become acceptant of ideas and blended our morality into something we can view as "tolerable" as a means of creating some semblance of societal coexistence...It's as if sin is only a minor infraction and since everyone does it, we must allow for it or become the legalistic Pharisees of the past...In essence, we have become the arbiters of sin. We, the self-appointed Guardians of Good...the Judges of Fairness and Equality. the near perfect, matured population that have moved far beyond the Garden...and we've done so by our own hand... We are each powerful agents of change that leave only goodness in our wake!

Some of us take an even higher view by comparing today's sin with that of other eras. To those, it's about the entire composition rather than our own unique time and place in the world. We tend to think we're all getting better and God has decided to relax the consequences so that we may all gain entrance to heaven... 'cause God is good like that...and surely the "wages of sin" have changed since that terrible, all-inclusive verse was written... You know the one... (It's at the bottom of this page if you don't)

I can only ask forgiveness for my part in the forwarding of that message. There are moments that I look at the sins of the world and compare my own sins...and I actually think to myself that I'm not as bad as all that. That thought in and of itself, is a sin... It's called self-righteousness... and rightfully, we deem this attitude "holier than thou." as if our sins are somehow removed from the others. That's the way of sin. It's disguised as something others do... because we don't want to be accountable for it so we ignore the "little" sins and try not to commit the "big" ones.

Unfortunately, that's not the way God views sin. There's nothing God can't see and there is no sliding scale. God doesn't grade on the curve. We are measured by the same standard and we are all guilty of sin. We try to believe otherwise and reckon that if we live a good life, we'll go to heaven... because we are the ones who decide what does and doesn't count as sin and which ones will block our entrance into heaven.

That is the very blindness that restricts us from asking God to forgive our sins and turning from them. It's clever because it is concocted by the father of lies. You know him too. We accept that repentance isn't necessary if we've committed no sin, so we can continue to work our way to heaven unobstructed by our "misdemeanors" ...because God is too busy dealing with felonious big sins to see our minor indiscretions.

I am guilty of that sort of thinking...I am as guilty of sin as any other. I am woefully short of righteousness on my own. I need a

Savior…because of this… "All have sinned and fall short of the glory of God." (Romans 3:23) … ALL is me!… All is everyone!

Now, the good news… We have a way out! We have a way to victory over our sin!… God recognized our complete inability to govern ourselves. He saw our blindness and propensity to love ourselves more than Him. He understood that we were incapable of righteousness because of our inherent sin. He understood that the only way to reconcile humanity to Himself was to send a sacrifice that would restore our relationship to Him.

He sent His son, Jesus to do just that. He died so that we might live. He took on each of our sins and suffered a death He could have avoided. After all, "In Him dwelt the fullness of the Godhead bodily." (Colossians 2:9) Instead, He hung there and experienced death without ever committing any of those sins we inevitably commit. He was the only sacrifice that could have reconciled us. He loved us that much! We cannot reconcile ourselves. We need Jesus!

> *Romans 6:23*
> *For the wages of sin is death, but the free gift of God is eternal life in Christ Jesus our Lord.*

Presence!

It is a beautiful morning here in Florida. Everything is blooming!...The colors are almost blinding...The sounds of the birds are everywhere (most of them probably foreign to those from other areas)...The honeysuckle smells permeate the air on the porch...The ceiling fans move it around...The coffee pot is gurgling and I can hear my wife shuffling around in the kitchen...

I am so thankful for all that God has given me...the ability to see the color, hear the sounds, smell the fragrance of the morning...a best friend and confidant with which to share it...and some time alone with the Lord of all of it...Sometimes it is overwhelming... How can I possibly thank God for all of this? I can't really...but I can see his glory in every moment of it.

I am saddened by the many complaining people...Those that believe that all good things come from other sources...those that seek happiness in wealth or power...those that find it necessary to condemn so that they might advance...those who refuse to see the beauty that surrounds them choosing only to associate with the ugliness that strips away every sliver of hope.

I can only pray for those who find misery in every corner. I want for them the peace beyond understanding...I pray that they will have just one moment of time with the Lord...so that they might see his purpose for them...and the glorious future he holds in his hand...

The wonders of creation are a good place to start...Look at it... Smell it...Feel the air... Listen to God's voice...He's everywhere at once! Learn about him! He awaits...and desires your company!

> Job 12: 7-10
> *"But ask the animals, and they will teach you, or the birds of the air, and they will tell you; or speak to the earth, and it will teach you, or let the fish of the sea inform you. Which of all these does not know that the hand of the LORD has done this? In his hand is the life of every creature and the breath of all mankind."*

Baconism

I LIKE BACON...THAT DOESN'T mean I am "anti-beef"...I am not a radical "Baconist"...nor am I a "Beefophobe" or a "Chickophobe" ...I just prefer bacon for breakfast...as do many others...

Conversely, I am not "pro bacon" in the sense that I believe bacon should be a dietary requirement...I do not support the introduction of legislation that would require bacon to be a staple in every school lunch...nor do I believe there should be a fine imposed on those who do not partake of bacon. I am not an advocate of free bacon nor do I see any particular privilege in my personal bacon consumption.

You don't like bacon...In some parts of the world, bacon is prohibited...defined by some ancient, religious order to be unclean... and that is fine with me...if that is your preference...I don't regard you as inferior or demon possessed because you don't partake of bacon...and I accept completely, your right to control your bacon intake.

It's when you announce that I shouldn't be allowed to have bacon... or when you determine that pigs aren't happy and increase the price of bacon by demanding "free range pigs." or some other intrusive act...that you become intolerant...If you attempt to take the bacon by force...you become oppressive...If you prohibit the bacon and make laws against its consumption...you become tyrannical.

Understand that I will fight you to the death if you try to take my bacon...not just because I like bacon...rather because what follows could be the removal of ham...or pork loin...or hotdogs...and it would never end. If you successfully remove the bacon, you establish a precedent...which develops into an agenda. Then, what keeps you from using that same force to remove beef...then chicken...until meat is nothing more than a bygone protein source... remembered only by the older generation as a breakfast staple.

So... When it comes to bacon, I am pro-choice... which may upset your moral compass but it does absolutely zero to mine...Apples to apples. Know the difference...and for the record, it's probably best that you don't mess with the bacon...Those of us who partake do not fear you!

Dotage

YOU KNOW...I'M FORTUNATE to have a particularly healthy sense of humor...I can be serious when the occasion calls for it... but mostly, in my mind, I'm constantly churning up ways to make people laugh...It has served me well for the most part...except maybe in high school where I spent a lot of time "explaining" myself to those who claimed authority over me...I spent endless hours "learning my lesson" but was never really apologetic about it...

In the service...same sorta' thing...Nothing particularly mean spirited but entirely mischievous and quick to respond...not exactly a welcomed attribute in a place where discipline is central to the mission ...but I survived it...and sharpened my skills...

In places I've worked and in my own business, I've maintained that same sense of humor. I've worked at a church for nearly 15 years. I have nearly shredded my tongue, biting it time and again. so as not to offend the others or distract from the overall ministry.

I'm sure that I'll have to be careful in the nursing home because older folks don't have the bladder control, they used to...and I don't want to make the nurses and aides work too much there. They may start to pinch me in my sleep and stuff...or order "more tests for Mr. Drew until he shuts up..."

I can hear them saying "Check his pockets...Miss Ophelia's medicine is gone." or..."Who put raisins in the toilet?"...or..."Mr. Stan put mayonnaise in his I.V. bag again..."

yeah...I'll probably spend a lot of my golden years sedated...but that's okay...Many of my younger years were spent that way as well. Which just made we a wiser cracker...

I'm putting baseball cards on my wheelchair spokes, though... That's for sure...I want folks to know it's me coming down the hall!...

Out in the Thick of It

SITTING ON THE porch. Two ospreys spiraling upwards. One of them changes course and dives straight into the lake three feet from our dock...The other watches...Then a big splash. The blue heron on the dock starts to squawk loudly because the breakfast he'd been watching has just been stolen. Snoozing and losing, as it were.

He lets the osprey know it as the eagle swoops in. The osprey is forced to drop the goods in order to do battle with the eagle. Apparently, the fish is already dead because the other osprey swoops in and picks it up out of the water, as if the entire event had been practiced over and over. It sounds like she's laughing at the eagle as she flies off with the booty.

The scene settles down for a moment and I move to the side porch just in time to see the red shouldered hawk dropping out of the trees onto some unsuspecting prey...I can't be sure what it was but I think it was a baby squirrel. There were several playing and now they've all hidden themselves...At least for the moment.

Calm returns as quickly as the disruption began...All this within a span of just a couple of minutes.

It's like watching the National Geographic Channel around here. There's a constant culling of the animal population. Somehow the balance is maintained.

We can see from all the nests that the cycle is ongoing. More of just about everything is on the way. Spring is bringing new life... We ourselves are moving here to be a part of the celebration.

I do wish these thieves would leave my fish alone, though...But then they're just coming off the beds so there will be plenty for all of us. Soon, we will become part of the balance...More the predator than the prey...But still...

There be Demons!

WHEN I READ accounts of supernatural events or demonic activity, I can't help but think about the people whose lives have been wrecked by drugs and alcohol ...I've looked them in the eye and shook them by their shoulders to wake them...I've checked their pulse for signs of life...and even wiped the vomit from their "Jesus loves me" t- shirts...I've watched them crawl and beg and convulse...and yell out loud to anyone who would listen...I've screamed at them, ranted at them, prayed with them, hugged them, cried with them... only to get a blind stare in return...I've seen them committed, jailed and temporarily "rehabbed".. only to return to the source of their trouble...I've watched them die...some slowly...some abruptly...and some by their own hand.

You may not believe in demons...but I've talked to them. I know them by their names...Heroin, Ice, Meth, Crack, and even ol' Jack Daniels ...with street names... like the thugs that sell them... Demons all! Yeah, I've talked directly to them and I've seen them stare back at me through eyes that used to belong to a human. I've seen them smile that sardonic smile and talk from tongues dipped in arrogance and pride... Yeah... I've met some demons in places most people never go.

I know all of that because I should have been one of those consumed...Certainly there wasn't anything to stop me. I had an addictive personality, many friends with a desire to get high and innumerable sources for any drug I wanted...

But somewhere...always...there was a prayer for me...My dad's small church in Tucker Georgia prayed for me no matter where

I was...or what condition I was in... That is the reason I am alive today...No one can convince me otherwise.

Because, as a result of those prayers, a holy, righteous God, in his infinite grace and mercy, answered those pleas and salvaged a life...My life!...He yanked me from those demons who would surely have killed me...So...Out of gratitude for the life I have been given, I pray this prayer.

Dear God and Gracious heavenly Father,

I ask you to watch over all of those today who have been consumed by drugs. Give them a glimpse of your hope. Send angels to their side. Bring ministers of your love to them. Protect them from themselves and those who would cause them to harm themselves.

Dry up the source of their abuse and replace it with your love. Surround them with Godly people who will reach out to them. Give them this day, your daily bread. Keep them warm and safe. Deliver them from evil. Cause a spirit of conviction to fall over those who produce and distribute harmful drugs. Obstruct their work.

Guard our youth who walk the line...those that consider their drug use "recreational"...Help them to see the resulting pain and despair... Create in them a discernment that causes them to heed warning. Help them to draw closer to you... knowing that in turn, you will draw closer to them.

Bless the families and relieve the burdens addiction places on them. Help them to respond with love and action. Restore their hope. Give them wisdom to navigate the loss of their loved one and empower them to act against a powerful foe. Provide for them the peace beyond understanding...and an extra helping of love.

For those without families, we ask that you would teach us to welcome them into our own. Give us the proper attitude and protect us in our attempts to help them. Give us your spirit of love and forgiveness...Help us always to remember that "There but by the grace of God, go I."

In the precious name of Jesus,

Amen

I Am Not

I GUESS PEOPLE WHO don't know any better, think I bow my head and talk to myself. Some think I live in an imaginary world and repeat some mantra to a deity that I've created in my own mind. Still others, think that I'm weak because I'm dependent upon some great genie from a magic lamp that I rub from time to time. I've heard a lot of theories about the cause and effect of prayer. I've come to understand that more people believe in coincidence than believe in answered prayer. So, let me make a very rudimentary effort to clear that up.

I talk to God. I do it a lot, sometimes at great length, sometimes in short bursts, sometimes on my knees, sometimes lying down, sometimes driving, sometimes in the midst of a conversation, sometimes, in the morning and sometimes in the evening. God, by virtue of His omnipresence has made himself available to me, whenever and wherever I seek Him. I try to remember that and reciprocate by not avoiding him.

God has proven to be approachable, relevant, active and completely trustworthy. He is all that He says He will be. Studying and listening to God is the focus of my life. I value His word and seek His will above my own.

I'd venture to say that most folks treat God like a casual acquaintance or a last chance solution in desperate times. Their prayers are relegated to laundry lists of what they require. God has become an attraction, a place to get in line and have their hand stamped for the next great, completely pleasurable ride. No consequences, no actionable plans, no worries... God is good, ya know...

The truth is, I have no great wisdom or power on my own. I can't answer all the questions I have. I can't navigate all the troubles I see. I can't protect my family against enemies that disguise themselves as friends. The older I get, the more curious I become, and the more dependent I am on the Lord. That is the way of this life. That is the nature of submission. He is God. I am not!

There is an unseen hand that guides me. There is a still, small voice that directs me to the place I need to be. There is, as He said there would be, a place to rest in the arms of the only one who can take all my burdens and carry the heavy load.

I am grateful to God and I take every opportunity to tell Him so. I am His. I was bought for a price. He alone is worthy of my praise...

> *1 John 5:14-15*
> *"And this is the confidence that we have toward him, that if we ask anything according to his will, he hears us. And if we know that he hears us in whatever we ask, we know that we have the requests that we have asked of him."*

White History

TODAY, WE CELEBRATE those who endured trials and tribulations, victories and defeats, successes and failures.

...those who overcame poverty and relocation, misery and shame, suffering and loss.
...those who achieved in spite of overwhelming odds.
...those who rose above the hate and fear.
...those who would dare to question authority.
...those who took advantage of opportunity as it was presented.
...those who sought to be light in a world of darkness.
...those who taught, shielded and protected others.
...those who pursued a life of service to others...
...those who sought higher, holy ground...
...those who defended freedom with their lives...

Oh wait...You can find people like that in every race...

My bad!

> - *Romans 12:3*
> *"For by the grace given to me I say to everyone among you not to think of himself more highly than he ought to think, but to think with sober judgment, each according to the measure of faith that God has assigned.*

Game of Bones

IF YOU'RE AS old as I am (and you're probably not) the thought of American people gathering together to watch a game prefaced by disrespecting the American flag, is so disgusting that watching it would be tantamount to accepting a total disregard for that flag and all those who paid the ultimate price beneath its stars and stripes. I just can't abide that.

I reflect on the mornings I pledged allegiance to it as a child...I remember watching it unfurl as we raised it over our school and played "To the colors" ... I remember the National Anthem was the last thing we heard when the T. V. went silent at night. I recall with pride, saluting it daily while serving under it...I also remember the many funerals I attended for those who valiantly defended it. Those memories don't just go away. I have no place to tuck them when others "protest." I have no reason to forget.

I hear others justify it..."It's just a protest to call attention to a cause that others see as more important than any flag." or "It's just a game. ".. "It's my right to protest! " But in the end, the disrespect of the flag has been ruled acceptable by the National Football League and like it or not, by watching that or any other NFL game, I too would be supporting that cause. I cannot, under any circumstances, support any cause that uses the American flag as a means of protest.

When the flag is displayed and the anthem sung, it's a time when I can actually "support the troops" that serve...It makes that cause more than just a bumper sticker. That same flag flies all over the world, in places most of us will never see...nor would we want to.

Our American children stand under that banner between us and any who would dare to cause us harm. Those are the ones with whom I stand!

Sure, some of our troops will watch the game on Armed Forces Television. There's ONE channel... and they would watch anything from home... anything that takes their mind off the task at hand, if even for a moment. All of them will salute that flag at the end of the day... but many will return home unable to do so. Some will see their last day on earth in a place they didn't choose, defending your right to join the protest...Think about that when the cameras pan to the "protesters" most of whom have spent their lives under the cause of nothing more than sport... and the money that comes with it.

Don't explain to me why it's okay to kneel during the American National anthem. Doing so, offends so many...families who have lost loved ones, those who have served and those who have family and friends in service now. How do I honor them and accept this pregame embarrassment?

This display of disrespect is a national disgrace and to just accept it as a temporary protest is to justify the cause itself. I can't find it in me to agree with a cause so dedicated to divisive displays and contemptible disregard for the symbol of freedom that is the American flag. That certainly isn't what that flag stands for... nor should that flag be held responsible for any such cause by malcontents who can't see past their own disgraceful actions.

How could I possibly accept any protest of the American flag and still honor those Americans who held her in high enough regard to die so the rest of us could remain free? It's the same flag flying over the stadium that's flying over outposts all over the world... not to mention every grave at Arlington. I simply cannot reconcile the difference between those grounds.

Certainly, you can disagree with me... In America you can do that. There's no faux outrage here. It may just be that I hold that flag in higher esteem than others. I get that... but to me... It's not just a flag... It's THE flag that has flown over countless fields of battle, been draped across so many coffins, and most importantly, it's been meticulously folded and handed over to far too many wives and mothers to hold as a memory of a life lost on behalf of this America.

So, pardon this old guy for standing when that flag is displayed and for singing far too loud when the anthem is played...and for turning off the T. V. when others align themselves with dishonoring my flag and my country...

I could no more watch the game than I could spit on that flag. It's just not something my bones will allow...Call me an over-zealous patriot... Call me a nationalist...call me a cantankerous old soul... but if the tide ever turns and I am forced to defend that flag with my last breath...Call me to arms!...

God bless America!

Eureka!

I KEEP SEEING REFERENCES to a "Grand Designer" a term used to explain anything that can't be explained in the universe...I guess that is an effort to keep from using the word God or heaven forbid, offering credence to any sort of faith in such an entity, as if that somehow validates his existence. I won't even bore you with any "new evidence" or foundational proof of the existence of God...Suffice to say that for now, the more scientists discover, the harder it is for them to hang onto some of their unprovable scientific theories...That is the way of theories...some make the cut...some don't!

Science isn't required in order to discover God...That would make science the arbiter of God...Pardon me for not getting excited...If scientists have discovered evidence of a "grand designer" ... all I can say is ...It took them long enough...

I know this about scientists...Consensus isn't built on a single discovery... nor are claims of "certainty" ever completely accepted by the scientific community until all schools of thought have been heard from and exhausted.

That is the way of the Darwinist's "survival of the fittest" theory. It's more of a self-fulfilling prophesy. From a single "discovery" comes many schools of thought culminating in many research grants...and much published results. It's an arduous process... doomed by a constantly changing creation rather than proven by its adherence to accepted consensus.

But let's just imagine for a moment that the entirety of the scientific community suddenly discovers the existence of God, on a level they could all understand and agree upon. They would then have happened upon what the bible refers to as "the faith of a mustard seed."...Recognizing God's existence is a pretty small matter when considering the vastness of his power and the expanse of his creation...

There is no reason to choose between God and science. He asks us to reason with him. That's the beauty of science...and the wonder of God... God loves science. He created it! God is a triune being. Science is an action...a study of a particular region of inquiry. The study of God is called theology. The two are not mutually exclusive. Many who study science come to a saving knowledge of Jesus, so there is hope even in the effort to understand the universe.

God is who He says He is...Read about Him...Seek Him... Discover him!

> -Job 38:4-30
> *"Where were you when I laid the foundation of the earth? Tell me, if you have understanding. Who determined its measurements–surely you know! Or who stretched the line upon it? On what were its bases sunk, or who laid its cornerstone, when the morning stars sang together and all the sons of God shouted for joy? "Or who shut in the sea with doors when it burst out from the womb...*

Introspection

IT'S HARD FOR me to look at me and know what others see... but I do hope they see that I am kind. I'm not always respectful of those who tend to be condescending. I probably don't give them enough space. I've been working on that for over 60 years so I'm probably about as good at it as I am going to get!

I would hope that others would see that I'm generous and caring. Sometimes that gets hidden in the "I will kill you where you stand" commentary. I would also hope that they would see the bulge in my pocket and make good decisions about whether it is a good idea to get physical with myself or my family. I'm cool...Are you?

Hopefully, people see a happy person, comfortable in their own skin, older and wiser...easy to talk to but no one's fool...Hopefully.

I'm sure they are somewhat reticent to engage someone with such a broad scowl. That, in and of itself is fair warning...It means I don't really care what I look like when our encounter is over...It's also a way I check your response... So yeah, there's a reason for it.

I have a nice smile...If is the best plastic prosthesis money can buy...I use it to let you know that I am pleased...I also use it to let you know I don't fear buying another set if you choose to break these.

I don't think the cane is permanent but for now it is a weapon of mass destruction if anyone needs it to be... I'm about as crippled as any other trained ninja. I gots skills!

I would hope people would see that I have a genuine love for people. I genuinely love for people to respect my space and that of my family. I genuinely love for people to respect my advancing age; I genuinely love for people to respect my property. I genuinely love for people to respect my opinion as I will theirs...So, my love is genuine.

I love my country. That won't change. You may continue with your protest against whatever ails you...but it wasn't me...or my flag...or my country...so learn some respect.

I am grateful to God for my life and everything that goes with it... because He created it and has every control over it. I love Him for His patience with me and because He bought me with His life.

Mostly, I hope that when you see me, you see a little bit of Him...I hope that my life puts Him on display. I have my moments but I try to live in such a way as to give Him the glory for any goodness you might see in me.

When I look at me, I know that I fail more often than not. Still, He loves me and I Him. I trust that I stay within the lines He has drawn for me and that I will be the blessing to others for which He designed me.

The process of improvement continues. However, it does concern me that more and more of my original parts are replaceable. I sometimes wonder if I'm being rebuilt for some greater purpose. Indeed, I am worth increasingly more... if only for salvage...

2 Corinthians 13:5
Examine yourselves, to see whether you are in the faith. Test yourselves. Or do you not realize this about yourselves, that Jesus Christ is in you? — unless indeed you fail to meet the test!

Purposed!

"You are fearfully and wonderfully made!" The design of your body is so complex that even your ability to read and process this is a miracle from God! You have superpowers! You can think and remember and plan and retain information. You breathe and blink and hear and talk...You are, in a word...AWESOME!

Disclaimer: A few things you're not...You're not a result of protoplasmic spillage...or mutant algae...or an accidental chemical explosion that slowly formed over a bazillion years... or a tadpole that learned to walk ...You are in fact, handmade...All the science in the world won't change that...because all the science in the world can't build a you!

It takes more faith to accept all of that science fiction than it does to accept the pure genius of creation evidenced by a single strand of your DNA! ...You are unique...You are a created being above the animals...above the angels...

God made you for His purposes. He loves you and has a plan for you! He has given you everything you need to perform those tasks for which you are designed. Your purpose is to honor him...

> -Ephesians 2:10
> *"For we are his workmanship, created in Christ Jesus for good works, which God prepared beforehand, that we should walk in them."*

The Compromise.

I'M NOT MAKING friends like I used to. I probably need to rethink a few things and get on board the peace train. I guess it's time to reel in all that Bible quoting. Who wants to hear that anymore? ...I really need to tone down all the Jesus stuff because so many are offended. It's so unattractive. All that "dying on the cross for my sins" stuff is just not polite conversation anymore. Yeah, I should just back off from all that!

I should probably never bow my head at the table in public anymore either because that's an obvious sign of a "holier than thou" attitude...or "virtue signaling" as it is now so cleverly defined. and I can hear people grumble when I do it. So yeah, I'll just skip that. It's so old fashioned anyway.

I probably shouldn't go to church anymore either because the crazies may shoot it up or light it on fire. I can use the money I save on tithing to help those people who really need the money... or give it to some help organization like Planned Parenthood or one of those. I don't give that much anyway and God certainly doesn't need my money.

I can use that morning devotion time I spend to help my wife with breakfast or wash the car before it gets too hot. I don't think God is listening anyway... The world is just going to hell in a handbasket. Nothing I pray for ever happens the way I want. So, I can take that off the list as well.

I've read the Bible enough and it's just not necessary anymore. I already know what it says so I'm wasting my time with that...It pretty much just says we're all sinners and can't be fixed so why bother since Jesus is gonna come back and fix it anyway?

I've talked to my family till I'm blue in the face about doing good but they don't listen. I'll keep praying for them when no one is looking. I don't know what else to do. My kids are doing okay in school and my wife is still in remission, so I guess God hears me sometimes but they don't have to know.

I can't possibly bring up the subject of hell around my friends anymore because that's just so hard to accept... People don't want to hear about that at all and to speak of it as an actual consequence sounds like something from a horror movie. We can talk about heaven though... Everybody believes in heaven because it's where we go when we die... you know 'cause God loves us all and that's all that matters.

I'm going to stop talking about Satan, too. People don't believe in him anymore either. That's just stuff people made up to scare kids into doing the right thing so I think it's time to put him up there with the Tooth Fairy and the Easter Bunny. The kids are old enough now so they know not to believe all that.

Yeah... I want to look smarter and get ahead in life. I really need to change my thinking. I'm sure my friends will appreciate it. There's so few of them left. Maybe they'll come back if I just stop all the preaching and talk more about love and peace and stuff...But wait...

> Psalm 119:1-4
> "Joyful are people of integrity, who follow the instructions of the LORD. Joyful are those who

obey His laws and search for Him with all their hearts. They do not compromise with evil, and they walk only in His paths. You have charged us to keep Your commandments carefully"

Small World

I decided that I'd make a world,
as real as any other.
I gathered all the things I'd need
From mostly basement clutter.

I fashioned all the mountains,
Meadows, fields and flowers too.
From the nothings I had gathered
I made it all like new.

I made a little walking man
Of dirt and sticks and clay.
I made it so he'd bend and stoop.
So, he could run and play.

I gave him camera eyes
So, he could see the world around.
I put on tiny earphones
So, he could hear the sounds.

I planted in him deep, a ticking watch
So, he could know
That I would always be a friend
Wherever he would go.

And finally, I formed his mouth
So he could talk and say
The long-awaited words to thank
And offer me his praise.

Instead he looked to me and said,
"I cannot see you there.
You're much too large and far away.
You can't exist," he shared.

"How can you say that I'm not here?
Look over at that tree...
I made that with my own two hands."
"That's science!" he decreed.

I showed him all the painted birds,
The cows, the horse and sheep.
The flowers in the fields arrayed
With colors his to keep.

I showed him all the cotton balls
I'd hung up in his sky.
He barely even noticed them
I could not fathom why.

He hung his head as if to pray
but slowly raised a fist.
Defiantly he raised it high
And yelled "You don't exist!"

"I gave you all the proof you need
Yet still you must reject
The very one that put you here
Why show such disrespect?"

I knew just then that nothing more
Would garner his attention.
I'd made a creature full of self
That needed intervention.

Imagine now that God,
Who formed us all from earthly dust.
With mighty, loving hands
He asks us only for our trust.

We point in all directions as we
Move about His space.
We keep Him at an arm's length,
Never seeking once, His face.

Thank God He's slow to anger
As we all praise one another.
And pat ourselves upon our backs
With each new thing discovered.

How God must look upon us all
As we, His people seek
Ourselves above all else without
Our list'ning to Him speak.

From deep within the forest
And high on mountain peaks.
From precious children's laughter
From shadows dark, He speaks.

Proclaiming loud his presence
From the place we call "On high"
If any of us call to Him,
He draws us to Him, nigh.

So, look around, you'll see Him
Sometimes it's just a nod.
But if you look more closely...
Behold, Creator God!

Post Mortem

I HEAR A LOUD creaking sound as I push open the lid. I reach outside of the box and grab the handle on the side. I'm too weak to pull myself up so I begin to rock back and forth in an effort to make the pine box fall from the stand... Nothing...I have no strength left. It's almost over...Soon, I will see the ferryman and take the trip across the Styx...

I scream for my wife but she can't hear me over my wheezing. The effort makes me start to cough again... over and over... my stomach muscles ache from the nearly constant hacking. The sweat on my pillow turns cold. I am sure I won't see the morning without a miracle... or an exorcism.

The double sneeze jerks the remote from my hand. It lands amid the used tissues and various half-filled drinking cups. Everything spills just enough to make the mess embarrassing. She comes in to see what caused all the racket. I give her the beaten puppy face in hopes that she will clean up the mess and I won't be forced from my certain-death bed to perform such a menial task. After all, without some miracle, I'm doomed for sure.

"Stan... It's a bad cold," she says, trying to sound maternal without being condescending..."Do you want more juice?"

I can't respond beyond my usual thumbs up... the endless coughing racking my body like a 7th century stoning. She brings the cart of medicines and I choose the one most likely to cause me to sleep... then one for the coughing... and one to dry up the fluids that continue to fill every orifice. She takes back two of my choices and watches me drink the juice that helps the medicine work its way down my inflamed throat.

"Get some rest," she says...

"Bumphnicken bluhbbanush... hnnnnnny" my final words through the crusty bubbles that have formed on my mustache and beard.

She knows what I mean...She remembers the language from the last time I died from a cold.

The War on Reason

REASON IS IMPOSSIBLE without God... Yeah...I said that... Unless one can reasonably disprove his existence or prove an alternative, then it is reasonable to assume that he exists... and... based on that knowledge, one could reasonably conclude that he is who he says he is.

Where do we look to find out who God says he is? Reasonably, we could conclude that he is defined in the pages of his inspired work...the bible...as it has withstood the test of time and has never been refuted on any reasonable basis outside of limited intellectual scrutiny...not to mention that it was written over 15 centuries by over 40 authors without one doctrinal discrepancy...No other book can make that claim. So, reason would discredit any denial of the Scriptures.

This begs the question "What is reason if not the ability to discern the very concept of a living, functioning God?" and..."Can man have a reasonable concept of the universe without a reasonable, substantiating, orderly God?"

Wouldn't it in fact, be unreasonable to dismiss those millions who have been changed over the centuries and who give account of his presence in their very lives through their study of the inspired word of God?

Wouldn't it be unreasonable to deny biblical events, particularly the resurrection of Jesus Christ, (since it is the foundational event of Christianity) if there is more historic evidence of that event than there is the entire life of Julius Caesar?

Reason without God is merely human speculation...limited by a finite mind and a rebellious heart that lacks any discernment provided by him...

Reason that includes God, is acceptant of a higher authority... deferring to a divinely created order, rather than a self generated definition of all that exists. Accepting that God's ways are higher than our ways points to a more reasonable view of an orderly universe. When we attempt to reason God out of the picture, we in fact prove that without him, our lives are meaningless and our existence ...unreasonable.

> *Isaiah 1:18*
> *"Come now, let us reason together says the Lord:*
> *Though your sins be as scarlet, they shall be as*
> *white as snow. Though they be red like crimson,*
> *they shall be as wool."*

Prodigals

IF I HAVE any single fault that is most obvious to me and I'm sure to others. It is my total lack of patience with people who have no regard for their own personal responsibility. I disagree completely with any concept that declares the plight of any person or group of people as systemic or indeed impossible to overcome.

The argument is "You aren't whatever (insert color, creed, religion etc.) so you can't possibly know."...as if life itself has been so kind and receptive to me that I never had a moment when it seemed the deck was stacked against me.

I guess the difference is, I accepted my failures as my failures. There were many, many times that I didn't live up to the standards taught me by my parents, my teachers or my mentors.

I was rebellious in my youth, guilty of childish and certainly wayward acts but I always knew that those acts were outside the realm of an acceptable standard; acceptable being those self-imposed standards that were commensurate with my upbringing. I'm sure that my family was embarrassed and or disappointed on more than one occasion.

As I matured (not just grew older) I was able to talk with my dad about this rebellious nature, if for no other reason than to determine if I was unique in some way...if in fact, my condition was irreparable.

I will never forget his response. He explained his own rebellious nature even going into detail about his lifestyle and his stories of being a drummer in the Big Band era. He began to tell me about his experiences. I didn't know any of this because to me, he'd always been a pillar of the community, a devout Christian and bible teacher... I couldn't believe what I was hearing. He laid out a picture of his own rebellious youth.

He even told me of a time when he sat in with Lionel Hampton at Jennings Rose Room in Atlanta, in the 1940's (That according to his memory...He wasn't sure of the place but he was sure of the event. I do remember the Rose Room sign) ...and how they all partook of the various accompaniments that enhanced their musical abilities (if you know what I mean) He said he loved beer "better than a hog loves slop." I had no idea. He never drank. My jaw dropped! We shared that love of barley and hops...

What he didn't know was that I frequented that same club, only the name had changed to "Richards." I spent a lot of time there. I found it interesting that he and I frequented the same club, 30 years apart.

He went on to tell me how he and my mother were members of a motorcycle club called "The 13 club." He was the 13th member. My mother verified this and told me in detail about the surgery she had to have as a result of the constant vibration from riding on the back of a 1948 Indian.

I was flabbergasted to say the least. He continued to tell me about his metamorphosis. You see, my grandfather was a preacher, and my dad a devout bible teacher. He was raised in the "nurture and admonition of the Lord"...as was I. Church wasn't an occasional visit and a handshake then...It was a necessary part of life.

My dad explained how he always knew of his own failures. He also recognized his own blessings. He came to the realization that his failures were not against other people, not even his own father. Those were mere disappointments. His failure was not meeting the standards he was taught. His rebellion was caused from his own human nature. His subsequent failures were consequences...the consequences of sin against a holy and righteous God...something those who have little understanding of such things, simply cannot accept so they blame their own envvironment, be it government or society or even their inability to be accepted by others.

I can't explain how those truths changed my life. Once I realized that God had expectations, I began to read about them. I began to expose myself to sound teaching and what it meant to follow Jesus.

The more I learned, the more assistance I needed from heaven. The more assistance I received, the more determined I became to follow the path He had laid out for me. The more I did that, the more I realized that Jesus had wanted me to follow him...to keep me from my own destructive path.

The world was attractive to me...I overindulged in all of its attractions...I was a failed musician as was my father before me. I failed at home and at jobs and relationships. The deck was surely stacked...or so it seemed.

I can't imagine how any change in me can be explained away except through the love and forgiveness offered me by my earthly father who taught me...and my heavenly Father who continues to love me beyond my own capacity for understanding. But the wages of sin haven't changed. Separation from God is the result of our disobedience. It is what it is.

Today, years after my father's passing, I endeavor to lead a life of gratitude. thankful to a loving Father who sent His Son to die so that I might be forgiven, victorious over the sin that so easily besets me...How could I not be accountable for my sins against Him?

I still fail, most often due to my still rebellious heart...but God is always there to pick me up out of the weeds and set it all right again...as He did with my father before me...and his father before him.

Jesus is who He says He is ...the way, the truth and the life...You have my word on it...and His!

> *Isaiah 53:6*
> *"All we like sheep have gone astray; we have turned everyone to his own way; and the LORD hath laid on him the iniquity of us all."*
>
> *Ephesians 6:4*
> *"And, ye fathers [and mothers], provoke not your children... but bring them up in the nurture and admonition of the Lord"*

Bear to Cross

HE DOESN'T JUDGE you or anyone else. He isn't hard on you and doesn't make demands on your time. He's mostly silent and you like it that way. You never speak his name in a public place or openly acknowledge his existence. You only have to talk to him when you're in trouble.

He loves you. He loves everybody...because that's what he does. He's not loud or imposing because he isn't rude like that. When a discussion comes up about him, you feel uncomfortable and announce that your relationship with him is between you and him. Its "personal."

You don't tell your friends about him because that would be awkward. He protects you at night while you sleep. He's always there for you but he doesn't control your life. He doesn't really care where you go, how you act or what you do. He laughs at your jokes no matter how "colorful."

He forgives you without your having to ask. You don't have to answer to him. He is tolerant and not at all possessive. When bad things happen, you ask him to fix them. Sometimes he does.

Teddy bears are awesome!... when you're a kid... You can't trust in them forever, though...

> -1 Corinthians 13:11 (NIV)
> "When I was a child, I talked like a child, I thought like a child, I reasoned like a child. When I became a man, I put the ways of childhood behind me.

Eight

I WAS STILL PICKIN' dirt clods and grass outta' my hair, counting my fingers and my blessings all at once... kinda shufflin' down what appeared to be a country road... Still, it was odd that I couldn't see my truck anywhere... I guess I missed the tractor trailer that was skiddin' sideways. I couldn't have missed it by much...but when I looked back there was just a whole lotta' nothin'...fog mostly... I just kept walkin'... My phone was nowhere to be found but I knew I needed to call my wife and tell her I'd be late...

I noticed right off that there wasn't any wind for some reason... and the skies were clear...also odd considering the weather the last few days. The road ahead sorta' glistened, like it had rained recently. The air smelled almost honeysuckle sweet... crisp and clean. I decided to just keep walkin'. There weren't any side roads or at least I couldn't see any but I figured I'd find somethin' before too long... I wasn't really tired so the walk was kinda' nice. I did notice my limp was gone so that was new.

I heard someone whistling. I had to squint into the light ahead but I could make out a guy comin' toward me...kinda' tall, zippin' up his windbreaker. I laughed because he reminded me of my dad. As he got closer, the whole thing started to come together...I was either dreamin' or I had traveled further than I'd expected...

"Dad?... DAD?

He picked me up like I was eight years old and rode me on his shoulders...like he did at the parades when I was a kid. I figured then that I must be dreaming... I was probably in the hospital...

probably busted up pretty good and the doctors were keeping me sedated. I must not have missed the semi. I didn't remember any of it but I figured I may as well enjoy the down time.

Dad just kept me up there on his shoulders and didn't say much... just whistled...I'm sure it was a hymn... After all, he knew all of them. I was enjoyin' the ride. I knew I was dreaming so I just sorta took it all in... I could see the outline of a building in the distance. Very bright... beautifully silhouetted against a pink and blue sky... As we got closer, I could see that there were a lot of people gathered...singin' songs I'd never heard...new songs. The singin' grew louder as we approached the now visible city... It seemed to fill the air itself.

It was indeed a beautiful city. We entered through some very large, very polished gates. I could see all around from my perch. Ahead, a great banquet hall. There were lots of people eating at long wooden tables, each with a perfect, floral centerpiece.

Some of the folks looked familiar...like family. Some of them waved as we entered. I recognized a lot of them... but my dad kept walking like he had a purpose. He walked me all the way up to the man sitting at the head of the table.

"Jesus," he said..."This is my son, Stan"

"Mine too! " Jesus replied... and he took me from my dad and hugged me...like I was eight years old. I saw his hands...I saw his nail scarred hands! I can't really describe the feeling I had in that moment.

It was like crawling up into the bed between your mom and dad after a bad dream... like when you were eight... It was safe...so much love... familiar... It was like...

"CLEAR!"...

Oh man... I wanted to stay...at least a while longer...

Someone whispered, "You'll be back soon enough"...It sounded just like my dad...

"We have a pulse, doctor..."

Credentials

Man, at counter: "Papers?"

Me: "I don't have any..."

Man: "What? You don't have anything that tells who you are? ..."

Me: "No... I'm sorry. I left everything in my pants at the hospital but..."

Man: "State your name First, Middle and Last."

Me: "William" Stanley" Drew"

Man: "Our records show you're already here..."

Me: "Junior...I'm a Junior, named after my dad..."

Man: Why didn't you say so?

Me: "Well, I'm kind of old so I dropped the Junior."

Man: "I see... What year were you born?"

Me: "1952"

Man: "Mothers name?"

Me: "Barbara...But she preferred Bobbie."

Man: "Okay, I found you... Says you're originally from Atlanta... What church did you go to?"

Me: "Sylvester, then Philadelphia, then Forest Hills, then..."

Man: "Okay... You're a Baptist then..."

Me: "Yes, for the most part..."

Man: "And you think you can just waltz in here and be all happy for eternity, just cause you're a Baptist?"

Me: "No sir... I believe I can come in because Jesus promised I could if I would trust Him...and I did because He died for me."

Man: "He did, did He? ..."

Me: "Yes sir, He also said that He came here to prepare a place for me..."

Man: "Do go on..."

Me: "... and that anyone who believed in Him would not perish but have everlasting life."

Man: "... and you believe that?"

Me: "Yes sir, I do."

Man: "Come on in, Stan"

Me: "Thank you, Jesus."

Jesus: "How'd you know it was me?"

Me: "I recognized your voice."

Jesus: (winks) "and I yours... Your family and friends are in the dining hall straight ahead...We'll visit later... Love you!"

Me: "Love you too!"

Jesus: ... "Next! ... Papers?"

> 1 John 5:13
> *"I write these things to you who believe in the name of the Son of God that you may know that you have eternal life."*

CPSIA information can be obtained
at www.ICGtesting.com
Printed in the USA
LVHW022030131020
668666LV00003B/225